ARNAUD DESJARDINS is among the most well-known and highly esteemed spiritual teachers in France. He came into the public eye with the success of his films on Hindu, Sufi, Tibetan and Zen spiritual traditions, filmed and produced for television, during the 1960s. Although he studied under various masters, it was the teachings of a Hindu swâmi in Bengal, India that most closely guided his steps along the "Way."

At present, he works directly with a relatively small group of people, whose number he keeps limited in order to have a personal relationship with each one.

He has published numerous books in French and this is the first to be published in English. A book on the life of Arnaud Desjardins was published in November, 1987 by La Table Ronde, Paris.

Kathleen Kennedy
Toulouse
France

Toward
The Fullness of Life
The Fullness of Love

ARNAUD DESJARDINS

TRANSLATED BY KATHLEEN KENNEDY

THRESHOLD BOOKS ~ 1990

PUTNEY AND BRATTLEBORO, VERMONT

Threshold Books is committed to publishing books of spiritual significance and high literary quality. Threshold Books have sewn bindings and are printed on acid-free paper.

We will be happy to send you a catalog.
Threshold Books, RD 4, Box 600, Putney, Vermont 05346 802-254-8300

ISBN 0-939660-31-8
Library of Congress Catalog Card Number 89-29542 CIP

Library of Congress Cataloging-in-Publication Data:

Desjardins, Arnaud.
        [Pour une vie réussie. English]
        Toward The Fullness of Life, The Fullness of Love. Arnaud Desjardins.
        184 p.
        ISBN 0-939660-31-8: $12.00
        1. Sex--Religious aspects. 2. Love--Religious aspects. 3. Success--
Religious aspects. I. Title.
BL65.S4D4713 1990
291.1'78357--dc20

Contents

"God created man in his image;
in the divine image he created him;
male and female He created them."
(Genesis I, 27)

INTRODUCTION

About fifteen years ago, when I was receiving many letters due to the success of my television programs, a woman who wished to know more on the subject of Tibetan masters came to see me at my home.

She looked about fifty years old, and was very elegantly dressed. I soon noticed that she avoided looking me in the eyes, crossed and uncrossed her legs too often, and punctuated her sentences with "Don't you think so?" and "So to speak." Why was she so ill at ease?

During our talk, I learned that she had read numerous books on the various kinds of spiritualities and met with the majority of "masters" known in France. No teaching had satisfied her, and she had been particularly disappointed in the people surrounding these "gurus," especially in the women who seemed to be closest to them.

"And yet," she insisted, "nothing else counts for me except this search for God." Her voice rose, as if to be more convincing. Suddenly, submerged in emotion, she cried out: "You must believe me! Knowledge is all I've ever searched for—not just any knowledge, no! Real Knowledge . . . Knowledge with a capital 'A' ." And she stopped abruptly. Freud himself couldn't have dreamed of a more revealing slip—nor such a painful one.

When I asked her to repeat what she had just said, she couldn't remember. So I repeated for her, "knowledge with a capital 'A' ," only to be greeted with a categorical denial. It was the confidence she claimed to have in me that finally led her to recognize her words. I then proposed she tell me the word beginning with "a" that one readily writes with a capital letter—again she couldn't. Seeing her confusion, I decided to back-track. Madame, it's surely not the same word for everyone . . . a young man dreams of Adventure . . . an old militant, of Anarchy. If you discover the word that concerns you, come back, and I'll be most happy to receive you." I never heard from her again.

Later, I told this story to a woman who had joined the small group of persons I was guiding on the "way of knowledge," in order to help her see the truth of her own aspirations. She listened attentively, and when I had finished, she inquired: "And so, what is the word?"

Filled with the memory of so much suffering, discovered little by little, with the passing days . . . the passing years, I have gathered, reviewed and corrected the typed-out pages of the talks which compose this book. The talks were given to small audiences, in an intimate context, to men and women whom I knew personally, and who had in common a previously awakened interest in what is generally called "spirituality" or the "traditional teachings." This book keeps the familiar style of those meetings.

In spite of ten years of "work on the self" in the Gurdjieff groups, followed by fifteen years of voyages in Asia where I studied with Hindu, Tibetan, Zen and Sufi masters, I never had to renounce my Christian baptism. Yet the sage who most closely guided my steps along the "Way," the one whose words most directly inspire my own words, was an Indian: Sri Swâmi Prajnanpad of Channa Ashram, (called "Swâmiji" in the text) not far from Burdwan in Bengal. The reader unfamiliar with Vedantic doctrine may be surprised to come upon Sanskrit terms in the following pages. They are given in reference for readers, notably those who practice yoga, who already have a personal knowledge of Hindu disciplehood (*sadhana*).

In the introduction to *For a Death Without Fear* (Pour une mort sans peur), I spoke of a volume to follow which would be called *For a Successful Life* (Pour une vie reussie). The reason I gave being that: "We are all the more ready to leave this earth behind once we have learned to consciously profit from 'terrestrial nourishment'." A successful death is the crowning of a successful life. And a successful life owes little to "success," be it professional, worldly, or financial.

A successful life is happy, fulfilled. Its fullness springs much more from what we are, than from what we have.

Nevertheless, whatever life gives, refuses or takes away from us also contributes to our ultimate fulfillment. One cannot deny that—even in the name of religion. Money does not bring happiness, yet only the rich know that. "Liberation" (in the Oriental, metaphysical sense) is never the fruit of frustration.

But my own experience—that of a man who has entered the secrets of hundreds of human hearts—has shown me that the profound frustration of my fellow man, be it latent or manifest, springs primarily from failure in love and sex. From the emptiness of solitude to the resentment of divided or badly-matched couples, I have heard almost daily the language of dashed hopes. Even more numerous have been the men and women whose sex lives seemed normal, and who themselves considered it so, yet who gradually admitted to me that it hadn't come up to their expectations.

Though the human mind be complex, even complicated, the truth is simple. Sexual attraction is the fundamental, universal law. No one escapes it, not even a monk or a nun. This all-powerful force controls the world but it can be refined, transmuted. However, such a transmutation is rare . . . and without it, we only end up rationalizing the errors. The choice is simple: you can go towards a normal, natural, comfortable love life . . . or you can choose a vivifying, also fulfilling asceticism . . . or else you can choose neurosis—perhaps only slight—but enough to eliminate any idea of living a successful life.

Many men and women, interested in or convinced by so-called esoteric doctrines, want to achieve a supra-normal state of consciousness. Yet they forget that one must first be normal. Everyone wants to love better, to make love better. But who loves? Who makes love? The union of a man and a woman could be a permanent celebration. But who can become childlike again, without simply becoming childish? To consider life as a permanent celebration of what is new, unexpected, marvellous . . . one must have the heart of a child as well as the maturity of an adult, capable of understanding and acting.

It is the simplicity of a successful life as a couple which, above all, makes for a successful life. But such success must be won. The talks which comprise this book can help the individual who wants to be happy and who understands that he attracts the destiny—and only that destiny—which corresponds to his own, deepest being. All the talks have a more or less apparent tie with sexual fulfillment. "Sex" implies the genital organs and the erotic zones, but it especially concerns a total human being—body, head and heart— a human being destined to receive, to give, and to transcend all dualities.

As a last point I wish to add that this book on the ideal couple does not describe my relationship with Denise Desjardins. It is rather meant as a homage to Swâmi Prajnanpad—a man born and educated in traditional India, who was so admirably able to bear witness to a conception of marriage increasingly misunderstood in the West.

Arnaud Desjardins

1

BE HAPPY

We have all heard the different commandments: "Do not kill," "Do not covet your neighbor's goods." Apart from the Ten Commandments of the Old Testament, there are many others in the different religions. But one day, at the end of my first stay with him in March 1965, I heard a really surprising commandment from the mouth of Swâmi Prajnanpad.

I had discovered India in 1959, and the Tibetan world in November 1964. I had therefore just spent some time with acknowledged rimpoches, when various signs, particularly during a stay with Mâ Anandamayî, led me to feel that the time had come to go and see a certain Swâmi whose address I had given to two acquaintances, but whom I myself had carefully managed to avoid. For sixteen years, I had been practicing different forms of yoga, meditation and vigilance. My stay with him (only two weeks) was rather short, but as Swâmiji was alone at the ashram, he received me for forty-five minutes in the morning and another forty-five minutes in the afternoon.

I had got it into my head that to receive a blessing from a sage was one thing, but when one actually met one's guru, one was supposed to receive an initiation in due form, complete with a "mantram," as described in René Guénon's books. I wanted Swâmiji to recognize me as his disciple. Needless to say, those ideas stemmed from the childishness of the ego that had decided that a guru and the label of "disciple" would give it more importance.

But Swâmiji eluded me. I therefore changed my technique and asked outright: "In place of a mantram, would Swâmiji give me one phrase to summarize all his teachings?" "Yes," he answered, "just before you leave, Swâmiji will give you the phrase." Ah, I was glad! The day of my departure approached, and after breakfast on the last morning, I went to say good-bye to Swâmiji, quite impressed to have met a sage who spoke English, answered all my questions, and gave such detailed and methodical teachings. Swâmiji announced: *"Now Swâmiji will give you the formula."* Just as I was leaving, he looked at me and said, quite solemnly, yet with a smile: *"Be happy, Arnaud."* That was all. *Be happy, Arnaud.*

I was not especially unhappy at the time. My professional life had considerably improved after years of hard times. I had developed a passion for my long trips to Asia and for the films I was making. Moreover, my free and adventuresome lifestyle as a filmmaker/explorer definitely pleased me. But at that: *"Be happy, Arnaud,"* I burst into sobs. It was so simple, so powerful, so terrible, that I felt it as a solemn commandment . . . no different from those Christ could have given his disciples or those God gave Moses for the Hebrews. And I was overwhelmed to see how fundamentally incapable I was of being happy.

I must admit I had not considered spiritual life in such a direct, simple way. I had thought of higher states of consciousness, of *samadhis*. Through my relationship with Mâ Anandamayî, I had sometimes even experienced what are called extraordinary states, though they did not last. My goal for sixteen years had been to be self-aware, vigilant, conscious, unified. But the words: *"Be happy, Arnaud "* were completely unexpected to me. I suddenly realized that I was not happy, even though I no longer felt the unhappiness that had been so very present at different periods of my life. I was not happy . . . What is more, I was altogether incapable of real happiness. And that, quite simply, was the goal of spirituality. I could not run away from him, or trick him. If I were to take Swâmiji seriously—and that I did—I could not forget those words.

I do not know if you feel and understand this as I do, but when a guru that you respect tells you: "Be happy," that is the most terrible of all commandments. And now it is my turn to give it to you. Do not dodge it; do not delude yourselves; do not lie to yourselves. In the book *A Grain of Wisdom* (*Un grain de sagesse*), I said that the goal of bringing up a child is not that he be well-mannered, or well-versed in the ways of the world, but that he be happy. That is all. Everything depends on that. You will never have problems with a happy child. All parents' difficulties with children come from the fact that the children are not happy. And an upbringing that does not produce happy children is one that has failed, even if those children enter engineering school at the age of eighteen.

But happiness is not only the goal in bringing up children, it is also the goal of the "Way." There you have a truly simple and accessible way of looking at "spiritual life." And that is the role of an ashram.

Be happy, Arnaud. I had not even thought of it by myself. In fact it had seemed to me very profane to be happy: only egoists and sensualists looked for happiness, whereas a man interested in spiritual fulfillment tried to be vigilant, to meditate, to unify his different tendencies and to awaken his latent energies.

***

Now I understand something else Swâmiji said, something I missed at the time. *"So miserable, so miserable"*. . . *"When Swâmiji saw that you were so miserable . . . "*. Indeed, what took the place of happiness for me back then were dependent joys and satisfactions. They depended on the success of my films, on my financial resources of the moment, on the conditions and circumstances in which I found myself.

Though I had arrived at a fragile and vulnerable accomplishment, deep down I realized that it was jeopardized daily by unforeseeable—though not impossible—events. And I knew that those dependent conditions determined my sense of peace and security. One could not really call that being happy. At most, it was feeling reassured, being carried away by joy, or by the heat of the action.

Be happy. The Gospels say: "Love the Lord your God with your whole heart, your whole soul and your whole mind." This is the first and greatest commandment and the second resembles it: "Love your neighbor as yourself." So often when I think of those words: "This is the greatest commandment," Swâmiji's "Be happy" comes to my mind. That is the Greatest Commandment. It took all Swâmiji's radiance and power of conviction to convince me to actually make this the goal of my existence. I discovered within myself a great resistance and all sorts of insidiously false arguments in order to escape this commandment—as if it were not a high enough goal. After all, any fool can be happy, and there even exists an expression in French: "un imbécile heureux"—a happy fool. It is pathetic to seek spiritual fulfillment while evading the simple question of happiness. Pathetic and deceptive. You can use the most amazing words—beatitude, bliss, *ananda*—or even more philosophical terms like serenity, but it is all only playing with words. We live in a civilization that has deformed and betrayed this notion of happiness. Indeed we do use the word, but any old way and always in the sense of a happiness which is dependent. When *France Dimanche* runs the headline: "I will defend my newfound happiness, says Sheila," (a popular French singer), it obviously has nothing to do with Swâmiji's *"Be happy."* I have often heard it said that it is not possible to be both intelligent and happy. You get the impression that the more intelligent someone is (like Jean-Paul Sartre or Simone de Beauvoir), the more tormented he must be. But that amounts to turning your back on all spiritual teachings.

The truth is that the ego is thoroughly incapable of being happy. Non-dependent happiness grows as egoism diminishes. Do not take the word ego only in the technical Sanskrit sense of *ahamkara* (the awareness of separate individuality), as if you were dealing with a highly esoteric science. "Ego," *ahamkara* in Sanskrit, means "me" and it merely represents self-centeredness. You see, the word happiness is not flattering enough for the ego. No! It wants to be wise, to meditate, to have transcendental experiences, to succeed in one field or another. And why not in the spiritual field, rather than in studies, sports or a career? If you simply propose: *"Be happy,"* it will turn a deaf ear.

Unfortunately for the ego, on that day I was unable to turn a deaf ear, and I burst into sobs. I realized how ill-at-ease I still was, because instead of seeing that as an occasion to complain or to be the center of attraction, I was ashamed. This was all I had come to after sixteen years of searching. Even after writing and publishing two books on Mâ Anandamayî, Ramdas and Hindu ashrams, I was still not definitively happy.

I carried within myself painful depths—ones that were latent, repressed and momentarily anesthetized by the enthusiasm and excitement of professional success. My grand expeditions, life in ashrams, discovery of the Tibetan masters, female conquests . . . all of that made me forget I was not happy. So many human lives consist in trying to mask frustration through work, adventure or success in one area or another, but none of these efforts really manage to free us from the suffering we trail along deep inside. To me, suffering even seemed to be something grand and noble. So many unconscious motives, amply studied by psychologists, lead us to suffer. We all have a deeply-rooted, childish idea that if we suffer enough, we will attract the attention of Mom and Dad who do not love us enough, or do not have enough esteem for us, or even worse, admire our little brother or sister more than us. That heartfelt cry: "and me, and me . . . me too, me too!" comes from the conviction that suffering will somehow bring us something. But that is a subject I do not really want to go into. You see, it is not necessary to spend time with Swâmiji for that, nor in order to study the contradiction between every living being's inherent, fundamental desire to be at ease, content, happy and his unconscious desire to suffer . . . as if there were some advantage to it.

But on that day I also felt that Swâmiji's love-filled words held hope. With those parting words, he was offering me real hope, a subject I had not even touched on in my talks with him. Indeed, I had asked him about the Atman, meditation, vigilance, self-awareness, concentration, mind, idea-association . . . but not hope. And he gave me those last words: *"Be happy Arnaud,"* as if that was the most important of all, and I had forgotten. That was what Swâmiji was offering you, Arnaud. A sublime gift. That was where all his efforts, and mine, were to lead me. And at the same time, he was making a request of me: a sacred and solemn commandment.

I often measured myself against those words of Swâmiji, because it took me ten years to fulfill them and to become freely happy. So many times, even after meeting Swâmiji, I was once again overwhelmed by my unhappiness, my suffering. But now I could only see it as failure, one for which my success in other areas could no longer compensate. Between 1965 and 1973, I enjoyed success in many fields—the kinds of success fortune-tellers promise. But my real failure was this: there was no doubt that Ramdas was happy; there was no doubt that Swâmiji was happy . . . and there was no doubt that I was not.

All of you also need to hear those words and to realize that your unhappiness by no means makes you grow, ennobles you, or glorifies you. It is simply failure. The best way to measure your progress on the Way is to feel yourself getting closer to the moment you can say: "Yes, I am happy." Are you or not? The rest is just tricks of the ego: I have more concentration, more self-awareness, more vigilance, I am exploring the depths of my unconscious . . . None of that can ever hide the simple truth of: am I happy? And even: do I quite simply want to be happy, or is there still some part of me that finds glory in suffering, and thinks suffering will make me the center of attention and show my real worth?

In *In Search of the Miraculous*, Gurdjieff is quoted as saying: "Try to understand this apparent paradox: nothing can be acquired without suffering, but at the same time, you must give up your suffering. And that is what people are least ready to give up." I first read those words in 1950, even before going to India, and I thought a lot about them. I realized how unwilling I was to let go of the suffering I clung to. Two verses sung by Cherubim in Beaumarchais' *Marriage of Figaro* often came to my mind: "I want to suffer out my sorrow, and to find no consolation." That is it. Gurdjieff is right. I do not want to give up my suffering.

Then the years passed. I left Gurdjieff's teaching and experienced extraordinary joys (the highest I have ever known) with Mâ Anandamayî. After my first stay at her ashram in 1959, life showered me with success that I had formerly been refused, notably in the professional field. Gurdjieff's idea that we are least ready to give up our suffering faded into the background. But as in those intense moments of life when you live so many different feelings in a flash, Swâmiji's: *"Be happy"* brought it all back. No, Swâmiji, no! Don't ask me that! What you are asking is terrible!

Look deep into your heart. You will see something inside that purely and simply refuses the idea of finally being happy, even though you all very sincerely claim to have suffered enough. But if you had really had enough, I can assure you that you would suffer

no more. If you continue to suffer, it is because there are aspects
of yourself well-rooted in *chitta* (the mind) that, unknown to you
and in contempt of your superficial desire for happiness, want to
continue moaning. That is the reason why Swâmiji's words were
a promise, a fantastic gift . . . and a request that we cannot run away
from.

If you have any other goal on the Way, I can assure you that
you are cheating. You are definitely excusable and you are absolutely excused, but you are cheating. You have been marked by the
samskaras of past lives (or in any case, by those of this present life),
by wounds, parent's mistakes, tragedies. You have built your
balance of life, your inner world, on suffering. You are adapted to
suffering and grounded in suffering; deep down, the very idea of
renouncing suffering is incomprehensible to you.

***

One more illusion was collapsing. I did not even possess those
real qualities of a disciple which ancient requirements called ini-
tiatory qualifications. I had far too many completely human interests to merit being considered a disciple. Of course, I had been
persuaded of just the opposite ever since entering the Gurdjieff
groups at the age of twenty-four; it took me three or four years next
to Swâmiji to see the simple truth. A disciple is a man who is totally and deeply engaged in the pursuit of the supreme Goal, not
one with so many adjoining desires as I myself had. Moreover,
Swâmiji used to say that he had no disciples, only apprentice-
disciples. One day I asked Swâmiji: "But after all, why did Swâmiji
accept me?" Because, even if I were not a disciple, he was a guru.
First he answered: *"Because you came."* Indeed, I had at least had
that merit: I went to him, while hundreds or thousands of others
traveling all across India did not. One's being attracts the events
of one's life, and they did not attract hearing about Swâmi
Prajnanpad.

Because you came. I came, yes. I was alone at the ashram, very
alone, looking at the horizon, immobile for most of the day, "in

contemplation," as certain Hindus say. And then Swâmiji also answered me saying:

"*When Swâmiji saw that you were so miserable* . . . " What? That almost angered me. What was that? I have films that go on television during prime time, I have double-page features in the French *TV Guide, Télé 7 Jours,* I am finally earning money, my expeditions to Asia are most interesting, I love my two children . . . "When Swâmiji saw that you were so pitiful." Later on, those words touched me deeply. Swâmi Prajnanpad was seventy-four years old when I met him, and during the last years of his life, he took onto his shoulders the burden of nine Westerners, both men and women. When he saw that you were so miserable, so pitiful, this old man felt compassion. He could not refuse to help you.

I am now well aware that the superficial varnish, the glow of a few successes and a certain fervor for my work did not mask the existence, under the surface, of a being who was in conflict, wounded and ready to lose heart. Under it all, I was apparently happier—much happier—only because of the fact that all was going well. If, once more, events had gone badly for me, I would again have been pitiful. Swâmiji saw it immediately. That dynamism inside me at the time, and that faith, could not hide from his eyes the suppressed frustration and fear. There, indeed, were the "whitened sepulchres" that Christ had spoken of.

The "Way" or the "Path" proposes that you leave behind this suffering—simply, truly and completely—and finally be happy . . . but not happy simply because you succeed professionally, because you have found true love, or money falls on you from heaven, or you feel surrounded by different types of security. That is such dependent happiness that it cannot smother the fundamental fear we have of losing it. This fear is only more or less an anesthetic. Swâmiji used to say *stupefied,* like a kind of morphine, or the smoke that puts bees to sleep so you can steal their honey. No. Completely eradicate this suffering and the very possibility to suffer.

You can hear this on all levels, from that of *ananda* (bliss) or *amrit* (translated as immortality, or sometimes supreme bliss) to that word, so simple and so strong, also of Swâmiji, *at-ease-ness,* the fact of being really at ease, completely relaxed. This is what is offered to you. Otherwise, you try to cheat. You refuse the genuine Goal, and the ego tries to come and steal at the ashram something that interests it, something it can salvage for its own glorification.

I should add that for years I was so occupied with my own sufferings, or my own suffering, that I was hardly aware of the suffering of others. When one is unhappy, one has the impression others are happy. I thought all those who made interesting programs on television were happy, that all those who more or less managed to make a living were happy, and so on. Then, I was carried away by my success, my accomplishment, and my various undertakings—and that again blinded me to the suffering of my fellow man. There were more storms and torments, but with the aid of Swâmiji, I lived through them in a new way—with the understanding and the capacity to progress through the trials. Yet the battlefield of life, to use the language of the Gita—the terrain on which I was fighting against the "mind," and on which I was putting acquired experience into practice—occupied me entirely. Oh, I measured my egoism and my self-centeredness well . . . better and better, more and more painfully, but I was not really conscious of those around me. Me, me, me . . . that, you know, is the leitmotif of the ego.

As I progressed next to Swâmiji, that simple *Be happy* from the first stay took on more and more importance. This is what I can attain; this is what I am called to attain. It is not egoism, it is actually the only thing that will one day free you from egoism. You will really be delivered from yourself when you are finally happy. Conversely, you can only be happy insofar as your self-centeredness diminishes a little. That *be happy* will become the center of your practice sadhana. And then you will once again be unhappy; once again you will find life painful and difficult. That is your mistake, not your greatness, nor that which makes you worthy of pity. It shows you your weakness and scatters all your pretensions of being a great disciple. You can no longer delude yourself.

And I continued to travel with this fundamental question in the background: "Is he happy?" It had become my touchstone. Khalifa-Saheb-e-Sharikar, oh, he is a great Sufi master; he has a very deep look in his eyes. Is he happy? Yes. Kangyur Rimpoche—is he happy? Yes. Kalou Rimpoche, is he happy? Surely. Karmapa smiles so much that you cannot wonder about him for long; he smiles from morning to night, he must be happy. Khentsey Rimpoche, is he happy? Of course. Sufi Sahib de Maïmana? Certainly so. Ramdas was, there was no doubt. So were the disciples.

It was impressive for one who was rather used to moving in spiritual circles, as I was, to see how in a poor and rough country like Afghanistan, not only the Sufi masters but also the disciples could be happy, smiling and radiant.

***

By the time Swâmiji died, he had kept his promise—at least the one he had made to me. He had given me the secret of being happy, as well as the mastery of that secret. He had taught me how to use it. He freed me from my own suffering and then from that which had anesthetized those latent sufferings and painful memories, repressed in the unconscious.

Then something happened I had not thought very much about: I began to feel others' suffering, and to receive a share of the suffering of hundreds of persons. Today, I too can say that which Swâmiji once said: *so miserable.* Because you are so occupied with your own "problems," you cannot imagine the suffering of many of those who are here listening to me today. But who is really determined to leave it behind—and to do so as quickly as possible? One would think it an established fact that you are all destined to suffer and that there is no reason to escape this suffering. Whatever you may say, your actions and your behavior betray how little faith you have. Do you want to suffer or do you want to be happy? Can you hear the words: *"Be happy,"* or are they almost unbearable for you? I have been through it and I can understand what arises in you. The years pass, and I see some just as unhappy as before . . . their only subject of conversation with me is their own suffering. How long will it last? Fifteen years? Twenty years?

Why do you come here? To stop suffering and to at last decide to be happy. It is perfectly selfish to suffer. I wish you all could discover, as quickly as possible and in a way which feels intolerable: "my suffering is monstrously selfish." Me, me, me, me, me, me. It is this "me" who is Satan, this "me" who is the Wicked One, this "me" who is hell, and this "me" who is the prison. Suffering cannot say anything but "me." And on this background of suffering, all happiness cries out even louder: "me, me, me." "Me, my success; me, my loves; me, happy at last." The same selfishness and the same blindness. One day I truly felt that there was something intolerable, "beneath my dignity," as the Hindus say, in being unhappy. I could not continue that way. When this decision really arises from your depths, then hope also arises. Have you not had enough of wading through your suffering, going from one to another, or suffocating eight straight years in the same suffering— exactly the same one?

There is one point that should be very clear for you, really clear. It is the paradox Gurdjieff so well described to Ouspensky. Nothing can be gained without suffering. And yet at the same time you must give up your suffering—and that is what people are the least ready to give up. Both these statements are true. It is true that the Way implies a certain type of suffering . . . conscious suffering, suffering that always takes on meaning. The housewife who goes to market and has aching arms because of the heavy packages she carries, feels purely negative suffering. A body-builder who lifts weights feels the same muscular suffering in his arms, but for him, it is positive. It is this suffering—deliberate, accepted, conscious, and intentional—this is the suffering that has a goal. The Way is not for one who is soft, for the coward, or for the one who always looks for the easiest way out, trying to avoid all that costs him something. Yet you should also hear the other side of that truth: negative suffering, painful suffering, suffering that does not make anyone progress . . . throw that overboard as quickly as possible. Decide that it is enough. "Enough . . . enough to be really weary of it all," as a famous Buddhist citation says.

Do not confuse the two, nor make a mistake. Christ said, and how famous are his words: "Happy are those who weep, for they shall be comforted." But if you look around you, they will seem at first like some of the most deceptive words a demagogue or an impostor ever dared to utter. Thousands of Christians suffer, weep, and are not comforted. So why did Christ say those words, and what do they mean? Precisely, that there are two ways to suffer. In the just, unified, real way: I dare admit that I am suffering; I do not fight against it or deny it, and I even dare cry if conditions allow it to me. Cry, do not whine. Whining is not the disciple's weeping, but rather the whimpering of the ego that wants to revel in its suffering . . . and those cries will never be comforted. If you mistake their meaning, Christ's words are totally false. Happy are those who weep . . . those who really weep, those who live through their present suffering in a just and unified manner, those who acknowledge and who assume it. That is a disciple's suffering, in the knowledge that there is a price to pay to be free one day, and that certain buried conflicts must even be dug up. The possibilities for suffering that we carry within should be lived through and dissipated. And when all those deep wounds are dissolved, it is over. You are happy at last.

Some have the impression, from one or another of my remarks, that the ashram has no other justification than as a place of suffering. I did not say that. Neither did Swâmiji. Never forget the brief, sacred message that Swâmiji gave me when I asked him for a mantram. What does being free mean? Free from the very possibility to suffer.

***

Each one should look honestly for himself into his own heart. What are you? What do you want? And even though I have said and written: "You will have to pay the full price of freedom," understand well that it can only be a question of this intelligent suffering, illuminated by understanding. The suffering which you know has its place on the Way will lead you directly to freedom and happiness.

I cannot deny it: I never promised the Way would only be a bed of roses. I have seen that nowhere. Disciplehood is neither a

joke nor a pastime for amateurs. One of you recently said something important for me, because my affirmation: "I have seen that
nowhere," has one exception. It was the ashram of Swâmi Ramdas.
I suffered much at Mâ Anandamayi's ashram; I had some very
difficult moments with the Tibetans, and I knew even more difficult moments with Swâmiji. But during my two rather long stays
at Swâmi Ramdas's ashram, I had the impression it was paradise
on earth, from morning until night. Well, recently someone who
returned from Anandashram told me: "I was overwhelmed with
suffering there." There is no real ashram or monastery that does
not lead you through certain trials. It cannot be otherwise.

Yet this—which is real and which I will always uphold because
I am not here to lie to you or to cradle your dreams—should not,
and should in no case, blind you to the fundamental truth. The goal
of education is to produce happy children . . . no more. If that
education failed—if at sixteen or eighteen you are not happy—then,
in perpetual unbalance, you run after that happiness which should
be the very expression of your being, yet which escapes you. But
at least, if you are not normally and spontaneously happy, you come
here to receive and to give to yourself the education that you missed.
It is not by condemning your parents that you will solve anything,
but that is the fact. All right. The unaccomplished work must be
redone; a de-education will be necessary and then a new education. And that new education, which I myself received from Swâmiji,
has no other goal than to allow you to live out this great commandment: "Be happy."

To each of you, I give a challenge. What is it you want? To
be happy, or to continue suffering? Do you want to make the ashram
a place of martyrdom where each one compares his suffering: who
will be the one to have the most horrible recollections of the unconscious, the one to have suffered most between two visits here,
and the one who is "even more unhappy since he started coming
here"? An ashram is not a place where one only speaks of suffering, and where one entrenches oneself in one's suffering. Bring me
something else besides your rebellion, your doubts, your heartbreak,
your helplessness or little insignificant compensations. Look to those
who have attained a stable peace in heart and spirit—they do ex-

ist—and inspire yourself only from their accomplishment.

Happiness certainly does not signify that stupid state that takes the place of happiness today: excitement, emotions, getting carried away. These are only a drug; they are the fixed smile in advertisements of the ideal man or woman whose "happiness" comes from a new love or a new washing machine—as if the two were practically interchangeable. Profound happiness is a feeling, not an emotion, born from the real and just acceptance of suffering that has been lived through and conquered. It is a happiness which is neither light nor superficial, one that has a certain gravity. It is a stable happiness. But it is also a simple happiness.

The majority of you are incapable of this. First of all, because it is engraved in your unconscious that you have something to gain in suffering, that you will interest Mom, Dad or the Holy Virgin, and that it is bad or selfish to be happy. Each time, as a child, you imagined something that would make you happy, things went wrong. It is true that sometimes the happiness we wanted as children was actually incompatible with family necessities . . . like wanting to put all the shoes in the house into a full bathtub, to make boats of them. There I give you one of my personal memories. That was happiness. And it turned into catastrophe. My parents spoiled my happiness instead of sharing it, instead of participating in my wide-eyed joy and then showing me that the shoes would have to be dried . . . An adult's life, an adult's heart, are sometimes made up of a few accidents like those, especially if there were too many of them. Another time, I no longer remember at what age, I thought of putting on make-up. My mother had powder and lipstick, and I carefully applied them. And my father took that badly, very badly. A new happiness spoiled. Of course, you smile over little stories like those, but it is engraved in you to feel guilt even over simple joys. And think back on the moralistic speeches about the selfishness of happiness: "How can you be happy when there are orphaned children, children who are lepers, children who are blind . . . ?"

Swâmiji gave me another priceless gift. It took a guru of Swâmiji's caliber to give me such a gift, and yet it will seem insignificant to you: he taught me I had a right to all sorts of little daily happinesses. He used a word I have often shared with you—the

word *recreation*. Recreation re-creates our life forces, our capacity
to face existence, our fervor to carry through our own practice
sadhana as long as we need to put in conscious efforts to progress,
and as long as our spontaneity has not yet been established. Swâmiji
gave that word all its nobility. I consented to make it as precious
a part of the Way as meditation, fasting, prayer, controlling association of ideas, dividing the attention to maintain self-awareness,
and discriminating between the Real and the unreal.

Dare to allow yourselves pleasure. There are so many simple
little joys you should be able to offer yourselves, through love of
yourselves, without the slightest embarrassment or uneasiness. But
a background of incomprehension, a false conception of what is
good and what is bad, of what you do and what you do not do,
has made you incapable of these little familiar happinesses, while
waiting for Happiness in the singular. A "disciple" should know
how to be happy. It is a privilege, an opportunity given to us, as
human beings, in order to progress on the Way.

I will give you an example. Perhaps it will seem ridiculous
to you or perhaps it will strike an echo.

After receiving that word, re-creation, from Swâmiji, one day
I dared . . . dared after twenty years of spiritual research, ashrams
and monasteries . . . to allow myself pleasure. I'd had breakfast as
usual, and found myself in the streets of Paris (at the time, my job
led me to do much traveling). One hour after that breakfast, I felt
an urge to enter a café and order a large coffee with cream and two
croissants. It is less dangerous than asking for the tenth *pastis* (an
aperitif made from anise) of the afternoon, but I had already had
my breakfast, and that is just not done. Swâmiji's voice resounded
in me: *"Father says it is bad; Swâmiji says it is not bad."* And it took
all the weight of his power of conviction for me to actually believe
such words, so strong in me was the voice of Father: "this is good,
this is bad."

It is not bad. I will not jeopardize my health forever by having a second breakfast, nor will I unbalance the family budget and
deprive my children because I spend a little money. I went into the
café. I dared to give myself pleasure. I dared to be happy. And I
said: "A large coffee with cream and two croissants." I remember

it yet. The waiter asked: "Butter croissants?" and I had a second of doubt. Butter ones cost more . . . did I have the right? Yes, butter ones. Eighty centimes more . . . What audacity! But what a treat! A large coffee with cream and two croissants. But wait, there is more to the story . . . An hour and a half later, I felt like going back to a café and re-ordering: "A large coffee with cream and two croissants." Would I unbalance the family budget? No. Was I going to destroy my health? No. Yet it is not possible; I cannot do that—it is not worthy of a candidate-disciple. Yes it is: re-creation. So I had the coffee with cream, and two croissants. Three breakfasts in one morning! And with an absolutely clear conscience. It had taken Swâmiji and that word, re-creation, for me to do such a simple act. You smile, but I wonder how many of you know how to allow yourselves pleasure with the unified and happy heart of a child.

You are not sure that you have permission. A verse by Musset used to gnaw at me inside, saying about Heaven: " . . . it punished me, as if for a crime, for having tried to be happy." If I am happy, God will punish me. God does not accept my having any other happiness than absolute holiness. All human happiness is tainted with guilt because it turns me away from God. That is false. And it is even the opposite of what the Gospels teach. I dared to admit that I was not guilty and that, like a child, I could give myself pleasure without Mom and Dad dramatizing it: What? You ate six croissants this morning?

Re-creation. Learn to be simply happy. Forget how badly things went the day you put all the shoes of the apartment into the bathtub, and the day you were covered in lipstick and blue eye shadow. Decide to be happy. If you suffer, suffer consciously, with hope in your heart; feel it as a challenge given to you, that wading about in your own sufferings—overdoing and exaggerating them—is not worthy of you. It does not make you grow in stature and it does not make a disciple of you. The ashram is not a place where one comes to spread out one's sufferings and share them with others, but rather one where you come to be faithful to those terrible and magnificent words of Swâmiji: "Be happy Arnaud." They are terrible for the ego, because if we are really happy, the ego has disappeared. And do not forget that word: re-creation.

Know how to consider it a sacred activity, the same as entering a
church, the same as meditating. Look for what makes you happy.
And feel that the moments of joy are not moments when you are
betraying the Way.
    Instead, go into life as disciples. The happiness we are offered
today is tainted with the excitement and the intensity of sensations
that destroy your nerves. What we offer the young is pitiful. Try,
at least yourselves, to escape this madness that has become more
and more generalized. Do not go looking for unwholesome happiness, deceptive happiness and treacherous happiness that is really
the temptation Satan lures you by, the better to destroy you. But
it is not Satan who is luring you, the better to destroy you, when
you treat yourself to six butter croissants.

                                    ***

    There are no holidays any more. It is finished. Today we still
say "the holiday season," but what does it mean? A month of
overwork for shopkeepers, a week of abusive spending for most
people, and two binges of drinking on December 24 and 31. It is
sad. In India, there are constant festivals and holidays. And people
laugh. When have I spent really happy evenings, with "atmosphere," as we say? Certainly not the day I found myself stuck at a
New Year's party, with confetti and streamers . . . an unpleasant
memory. I have memories of feasts in Afghanistan, in the midst
of poor people, the songs at night, the fires in the desert . . . And
then, in the heart of the feast, it is time to pray. With the Tibetans,
where we even drank (like the "sake" in Zen monasteries) . . . feasts
where you really dared to become childlike again. Do you think
that celebrating is unworthy of a disciple? Nowadays, what we call
having fun means letting oneself be carried away by excitement.
It is sad that we can no longer even use the word celebration. It is
an essential element of every "right" civilization, and we have lost
even that.
    And to finish, to shock you even more, after having talked
of celebrating and eating croissants, I will use quite a profane image

that left me with a message. It is the ending of a film many of you may have seen—it is neither *The Life of St. Francis of Assisi* nor *The Message of the Tibetans* by Arnaud Desjardins—but a film, famous in its own time: *Never on Sunday*. Produced by a very great director, Jules Dassin, and starring Melina Mercouri, grand-daughter of the former mayor of Athens, the film portrays the life of the prostitutes of the port of Piraeus. It is the story of an amateur philosopher who went to live in the land of Socrates and Pythagoras (played by Dassin himself), who got it into his head to save one of these ladies. You recognize the theme of Pygmalion: turning an ignorant woman into an educated and refined one. And she believed it for a while. She thought it was bad to be a prostitute, and good to know literature and study Shakespeare.

So she lets herself be taught the "real values" of philosophy. But little by little, the situation is inverted. She begins to feel smothered in that bookish culture and, in a suggestive scene, while looking at a picture of a football team, she sings: "Eleven athletic men are worth all philosophies!" But the amateur philosopher, still up to his usual tricks, drives a local singer to despair by telling him: "If you cannot read notes, you are not a real musician." The singer immediately locks himself in the restroom of the little cabaret where he sings, and refuses to come out, declaring he would rather die. The prostitute suddenly has an ingenious idea: "Birds do not know how to read notes either" she tells him, "but everyone finds their singing wonderful." So he comes back to life. In the end, the philosopher finds himself surrounded by sailors, fishermen, and women of the street . . . he accepts glasses of alcohol, balances them on his head, and dances and dances, bending low and coming back up . . . and then he empties his glass and throws it across the café. He is the one who, after all, learns to relax, to be simple, to live, to dare feel something with his senses and with his heart. He participates in a joyous atmosphere that is not that of an ashram or a monastic community, but that of men and women who are still capable of a little truth and a little happiness. It is not he who saved the woman, but she who saved him.

I felt that I, personally, had a great lesson to learn from that film. Am I capable of being simply at ease like that—relaxed, happy,

unified—or do I always stand back, thinking: "I am a disciple; I am
on the Way; what kind of worldly, superficial pleasure is this? There
is nothing outside of monastic austerity." Oh, what folly! *Be happy,
be happy.* Come out of that suffering in which I see you struggling.
BE HAPPY. If you continue to advocate suffering (on the pretext—
and it is true—that a certain consciously-lived suffering is the price
to pay), then this ashram is no more than a betrayal of the truth, a
place to which I advise you never to return. People are unhappy
enough everywhere, without looking for even more unhappiness
here. Come here to be happy.

2

ACTION, EXPERIENCE, KNOWLEDGE

I happened to meet Swâmi Prajnanpad after numerous visits to India over a period of six years, during which I had often had conversations with sages, swâmis, pundits and experts in traditional knowledge. And many times, Swâmiji expressed truths that at the start seemed to totally contradict what I had heard repeatedly over those six years. It is surprising, for example, for a Christian to hear: "The most important of all is to love yourself."

There are three words that played a particularly important role in my conversations with Swâmiji.The first is *bhoga*, a word found in most books on Hinduism. It is usually translated by "enjoyment"—a term not very highly esteemed in spiritual language. I had always heard *bhoga* used severely and with criticism. It was as if the word indicated a fault or, in any case, a level of functioning characteristic of the ordinary man living in error, or in sin, a level renounced by one who embarks upon the spiritual way. All the usual Hindu writings seem to be unanimous in this view. It is acknowledged that man is unfortunately attracted by *bhoga*, but he who wishes to commit himself upon the Way turns aside from such sensitive, sensuous or even intellectual enjoyments, in order to search only for God or for the Absolute.

And then Swâmiji used that word *bhoga* with me, giving it instead an important and precious meaning—one just as precious as the word yoga. Here we have the heart of his teaching. He often cited for me a Sanskrit phrase from "Yoga Vasishtha"—"*Maha karta maha bhokta maha jnani bhavanagha*." Unless you are a *mahabhokta* (a great appreciator), you cannot be a *mahajnani* (a great sage), and unless you are a *mahakarta* (a great doer), you cannot be a *mahabhokta* (a great appreciator). Word for word, *maha karta* means "the great doer." *Maha bhokta* would perhaps be translated as "the great enjoyer," but after many years' reflection on the translation of that word, I prefer to say "the great appreciator." And *maha jnani* means "the great sage."

As a prior stage, Swâmiji used three other terms: *Karta* meaning "the doer" (*karta* has the same origin as the famous word karma—action); *bhokta* meaning "he who has the experience of things, the appreciator," and *jnani* meaning "he who knows." The word *jnani* is sometimes used to designate one who has achieved supreme Knowledge, but in the language of Yoga Vashishtha, *jnani* means he who has the right to speak of things because he knows them in themselves, as they are, not one who experiences things through his own idiosyncrasies, subjective vision and prejudices.

What, for a long time, rendered this situation quite confusing for me was that I had come to India in 1959, with ten years' experience of the Gurdjieff teachings to my account. If you read Ouspensky's book, *In Search of the Miraculous*, the psychological chapters very closely resemble Swâmiji's teachings. Gurdjieff insisted on certain phrases that were a relevation for me at the age of twenty-four: "Man does nothing, everything happens," "Modern man does not act; something acts through him." This is what Gurdjieff called the "man-machine." In place of the word "to act," this book uses the word "to do." "The only thing that is miraculous is the capacity to 'do'—to act freely, instead of to 'function,' to react like a marionette according to the chain of cause and effect."

Concentrating on vigilance, self-awareness and attention, I had done my best for years "to do," and therefore (although I did not use the word then) to become a doer, and no longer a machine. When you are not vigilant, you do not do; when you are vigilant—conscious that you "are"—you can also be conscious of what is happening within yourself, of what you say, of the actions you perform, and that is the way to become capable of "doing." Although the Gurdjieff teachings did not enable me to stop being a machine, they did at least convince me that I was one. We practiced a certain number of exercises that clearly showed us how we functioned, that we were not capable of acting freely, and that mechanisms over which we had practically no control reacted in us to circumstances, situations, and exterior stimuli.

Yet ever since my first trip to India in 1959, I had heard repeated here and there, in one ashram or in another, by a master or by a disciple, an expression which bewildered me: "Free from the 'I am the doer' illusion."

Ah! Now what is this? For ten years I have been trying to truly be the doer of my actions, and now I am being asked to be free from this illusion? In trying to better understand what this meant, I grasped that the illusion of being the doer of the action corresponded to that "ego" which I heard mentioned every day as a limitation that must be effaced. I must realize that, as an ego, I do not exist, that the sense of an individualized self is an illusion, and that it is only divine Energy, the Shakti, which acts and expresses Itself. How could I reconcile the efforts the Gurdjieff teachings required of me— efforts I had assiduously put into practice—with this ultimate teaching of the egoless state, with the discovery that it is not I who acts and that there is a pathological pride in believing that one is the doer of the action when we are only cells of the universal body of Nature?

The doer—that illusion that must be dropped—is called *karta* in Sanskrit. I had started to hear the word from time to time. However instead of their usual derogatory sense, Swâmiji gave the words *karta and bhokta* a new and fundamental meaning in his teaching. *Karta*—"the doer," *bhokta*—which I prefer to translate as "the appreciator," and *jnani*—"the sage": a whole book could be written on those three words.

However, Swâmiji made a distinction I had never heard until then, between *bhoga* and *upa-bhoga*. The word *upa* roughly means "not the real one." For example, you have a guru, and you can also have upa-gurus, but the upa-guru is not your real guru. *Patni* means wife; *upa-patni* is mistress. And *upa-bhoga* designates enjoyment which is not real appreciation. Swâmiji showed me that rather than trying to be free from *bhoga*—in a dream of Liberation that had led me nowhere, I would do better to first understand the difference between *upa-bhoga* and *bhoga*. This was also true for almost all the Indians or Europeans I had met here or there in ashrams.

***

Bhoga implies the real experience of total life—the result of a series of particular bhogas which are themselves the experience of a situation, whatever it may be. *Upa- bhoga* denotes experience that does not make one progress. Swâmiji showed me, through the many concrete life occurrences which I brought him, that the word bhoga was generally used for that which was actually *upa-bhoga*, a falsified—doubly falsified—existence.

One who is not yet a sage—who is still subject to the ego, moved by his demands, desires, and fears—feels the need to turn outward. He feels incomplete in himself and searches outside himself for that which he lacks. Yet, were he to discover the Self, he would see that he actually lacks nothing, that he already carries fullness within himself, that he is in the same situation as a man who has received everything, and to whom life has given everything. But because he has not discovered his essential nature, man

functions in the dualistic manner of attraction and repulsion, with a feeling of incompleteness and dissatisfaction. He seeks experiences, whether it be driving a car at 125 mph, conquering a new woman every week, being intoxicated with victory or political power, or even playing cards with his buddies at the local café.

The principle is the same on all levels: I cannot content myself with what I am, so I try to fill in this poverty of my being with acquiring, in one form or another. All right, that is the general law, let us admit it. But if we think it is possible to transcend this condition—which we would normally not even dream of doubting—let us start by realizing that it is nonetheless where we are now. And although *bhoga* can lead to Liberation, *upa-bhoga* never does. As long as, like a parrot, you repeat the beautiful words of swâmis on bhoga and yoga, you will be doing nothing but deluding and lying to yourself. For now, what you take to be *bhoga* is no more than *upa-bhoga*, the false appreciation of things. You can live, you can multiply your love affairs, conquests and exploits, but you do not have any real experience of them. Therefore you do not have the knowledge that liberates.

Your usual condition is to live "identified," in the same sense as Gurdjieff used the word. There is not a being aware of himself, aware that he is living and "doing." I do not have the right to say that I fulfill my desires, but only that my desires fulfill themselves. Unless I am completely distracted or in a dream, I am aware that I am eating, but I am not aware that "I am" and that I am eating. Only vigilance, *awareness*, can increase this capacity to consciously appreciate situations and experiences, or, quite simply, to consciously appreciate the fulfillment of a desire at the moment it happens.

Swâmiji used a very effective phrase: "Be there to consciously fulfill your desires, so that your desires will not fulfill themselves at your expense." Do not look on the word desire with guilt, even though a sage is said to be free from desire. The desire is there. *Who* feels the desire? *Who* decides to fulfill it? After examining all the ins and outs of the situation, all the parameters, *who* is fulfilling it? *Upa-bhoga* is unconscious fulfillment in which the subject is absorbed by the object.

Swâmiji said, *"There is no I"*; *"You are nowhere."* That seems obvious to you when you are completely carried away, when you rush to the telephone, without even taking five minutes to think before calling someone—to yell at him or to entreat him—caught up in great fury, deep despair or ardent passion. But this is also true in the ordinary circumstances of life, where events happen mechanically, without our consciously appreciating them. Try to always be there—present to yourself, present in yourself—in order to appreciate everything . . . even a simple thing, like eating a slice of bread and butter for breakfast.

As well as this fundamental necessity of self-awareness, I discovered another truth. The word *bhoga*—translated as enjoyment—means the total appreciation of one's destiny, of one's karma (not only the happy situations), and the total appreciation of the satisfaction of a desire while it is happening. But *bhoga* also means the appreciation of that which we normally consider unpleasant and which we would voluntarily do without. This is where I consider the translation of *bhoga* by *enjoyment* as unsatisfactory, because it eliminates the major aspect of comprehension.

When you see the word "enjoyment," you understand it to

mean eating well, making love, and spending a fortune to be the most elegant man in Paris. Or maybe you see it as something more simple and natural, like being with one's family and playing with the children. But it would not normally enter your mind that the word *bhoga* could apply to a severe case of colic. This is what degrades our approach to the immense knowledge that India has transmitted to us, and reduces its wealth to a few trite religious knick-knacks or to technical yogas which are not really within our reach, such as the real Hatha-Yoga described in the Hatha-Yoga-pradipika. *Bhoga* means experience or appreciation. Certain experts are capable of appreciating a famous vintage Bordeaux wine, but are they equally capable of appreciating a severe bout of renal colic? It is a very painful physical condition I once experienced.

Existence, as long as you live it in the ordinary state of consciousness, includes all we consider pleasant (which we qualify as happy), as well as all we consider unpleasant (which we call unfortunate, painful, disastrous or tragic). To truly be human on this planet—to evolve instead of mechanically reincarnating, driven by *vasanas* buried in the unconscious—one must become *bhokta, the conscious appreciator* of both aspects of reality: the pleasant aspect and the unpleasant aspect. This is difficult for you because it is written into each of your cells to refuse, on the spot, all that does not suit you. You let yourself be carried away by a negative emotion, and then you refuse the emotion itself. Or instead, you identify with your desires and your impulses. You do things without really enjoying them, because you do not consciously enjoy them in a state of vigilance or self-awareness.

Most happy moments are badly experienced because they are lived on a more or less unconscious background of guilt . . . as if you did not have the right to be happy. "How selfish to enjoy yourself when so many are suffering everywhere." We do not lessen others' suffering by refusing to live a happy situation to the fullest, here and now. No, we all know that the moments of joy will not last forever and that unfortunate circumstances will return. The very moment you are experiencing a happy situation—even one you desired—you experience it greedily, in order to enjoy it to the fullest. You do your best to smother the certainty engraved inside you that disappointment will return once again, and that, at any rate, this marvelous moment will not last.

***

Swâmiji's teaching developed year after year around personal obstacles—difficulties inherent in ourselves—many of which were a matter of pure and simple psychology. For each of us, and for me, Arnaud, in particular, the teachings revolved concretely around that which hindered me from truly being *bhokta*, the appreciator, and from fully living *bhoga*. What is it that hinders me? Why do I still let myself be carried away by situations and emotions? And why am I incapable of really appreciating painful situations? It is fundamental to understand this word *bhoga* in a new sense. It does not mean looking everywhere possible for pleasure. Rather, it is the real experience which can give you Knowledge.

Although *bhoga*—the real appreciation of both happy moments and painful ones—can lead little by little to Liberation, *upa-bhoga*— the greedy, impulsive manner of living, of seeking happy moments and fleeing painful ones—leads nowhere. It adds fuel to the flames. And everything said so critically about *bhoga* in Hindu literature or by certain masters, actually concerns *upa-bhoga*—false experience. The truth is contained in these two words. Starting there, we very often ask the impossible of ourselves. We want to act right away as if we were free from fears and desires—when we are not. Then there is no longer a Way, and all that is left is an illusion, a desperate dream, a fascination for the wisdom we see embodied in Ramdas or in Mâ Anandamayî. The years pass—five, ten, fifteen. We have the impression we are at a standstill, and then sooner or later we find that we are once again submerged in an inner crisis.

One cannot play with one's unconscious--one's drives, fears and desires. And one cannot play with the Way. "It is not a joke," said Swâmiji. You must be realistic and take cleverly into account all that you are today. If I content myself with dreaming of Wisdom, and with looking down on all that proves to me that I am

not yet a sage—I will get nowhere. I must be real, be true to myself as I am today, and make my life into a true Way, a progres-
sion. I must replace *upa-bhoga*, the habitual manner of living, with
bhoga, conscious experience.

There are two conditions for this. The first, which is not easy,
is to increase deliberate action. Observe situations; think them over.
This desire . . . will I fulfill it or not? Why do I want to fulfill it?
What do I want from it? What will be its eventual consequences?
Even if the consequences are not those I hoped for, at least I can
learn something . . . it is a lesson. What is startling, when you see
it with open eyes, is to what extent we human beings learn practically nothing in life. We know no more about it at sixty than at
twenty. We can "know," but I am not talking about knowing. By
reading and by acquiring diplomas, you can gain an immense
knowledge. But Knowledge, in the real sense of the word, is a
function of being. We know something because we embody it—
because it is in our blood.

How very little we learn from life! We are in love at twenty-
five, and at fifty-five, we are in love once more, according to the
same "pattern," as Swâmiji said. It is as if all our experiences had
taught us nothing. Man marks time and, even as he ages, he con-
tinues to function according to the same outlines, the same stereo-
types. This is the fault of *upa-bhoga*. Real appreciation constitutes
a Way in itself. Because of my austere Protestant education, because
I was permeated with a Hinduism I had misunderstood, this was
difficult for me to hear. Yet it must be heard if one does not intend
to deny the truth.

The second point is that you cannot appreciate life's happy
moments unless you know, deep inside, that you can also appreciate the painful ones, rather than refusing them with all your being.
Then you can feel free to completely take advantage of all that is
given to you, here and now. Otherwise, the happy moments are
but a compensation for the general fear in which you live, the fear
of suffering. To appreciate a painful situation is to be one with it,
to be one with the suffering. It is only in this way that we can learn
something.

One human existence can be enough for you to attain Wisdom—if that existence is used well. If you lose all opportunities to put this teaching into practice—to be a real appreciator—you will not progress and you will never discover the Self. Appreciate everything: sun and rain, health and sickness, little events to which you would not even pay attention, the cruel aspect of life.

If I am not able to appreciate a painful situation, I can at least appreciate the emotion of suffering that I am feeling. This is a new and revolutionary approach to the painful face of life. Never again say: "That's terrible"—rather say: "That's very interesting." You must manage it. Sooner or later, you will have to concretely arrive at the fact that this is not just a sentence spoken by Arnaud on a Sunday afternoon. If you really want it, if you have decided on it, you will succeed. You can bring about a complete change in that deeply-rooted attitude engraved in you. Cross "that's terrible" out of your vocabulary: "That is very interesting and very precious, for it will allow me to progress and to turn my existence into the fullness of human life, which leads naturally to Wisdom."

This process develops slowly, yet the reversal happens in an instant. I remember precisely the day which was the turning point in my life. It was not that I no longer had emotions, but rather that I viewed the entire future in a radically new light. Quick . . . let there be a painful situation so I can put into practice what I have just understood, and never more let it escape. For some forty years, I have been uselessly suffering because I have never known how to be a real appreciator, a real *bhokta* of that aspect of existence which we call suffering. We listen to this repeated a hundred times . . . and then one fine day, we hear it for the first time.

***

There was also the word *karta*, the doer. Although Swâmiji never used the word *upa-karta* with me (perhaps it does not exist in Sanskrit), this was a word implied in all his teaching. There is a mechanical, non-conscious way of acting, and there is a conscious way of acting. There are what we call reactions, and what we call actions. I could also say: "Be there to act, so that your actions will not fulfill themselves at your expense."

But it is interesting to understand the relationship between these two words: the appreciator and the doer. There must be an appreciator to appreciate—not simply mechanisms. There must be that state of alertness which Gurdjieff called *self-remembering* and which Swâmiji called *awareness*. Appreciating suffering or appreciating joy is also an action. The word *karma* is very general, for even a thought is an action—a mental action, a psychic action. There must be a *karta*, a doer, who is there to accomplish the particular action of appreciating a situation, in order to obtain its real experience . . . unfalsified by the mind and the ego. But conversely, you cannot generally speaking be a doer unless you have the experience which gives a right appreciation of all aspects of existence, the happy aspects and the painful aspects. Little by little, you will be less imprisoned by the opposition between that which you like—and want at all costs—and that which frightens you, and which you refuse, also at all costs. As long as you are controlled by this duality, you cannot be a doer. You have not accepted living in the real world, and whatever the cost, you want to superimpose your world—the world as it should be—onto the world as it is.

That is why the majority of people—even those who have succeeded in business, politics or love—remain machines, as Gurdjieff so cruelly said. Their actions are not objective. They do not respond to reality perceived objectively, to what situations require. Their actions express a deep-seated mechanism: I want what I like; I do not want what I do not like. Only a *bhokta*—one who has real knowledge of total existence—can act truly, instead of reacting. It is no longer simply his emotional mechanisms and his ego which are at work.

The *karta* becomes the appreciator because there is someone there to appreciate. And the appreciator becomes the doer because there is someone there to face life as it is—instead of life as he wishes it were, experienced through his mind and his projections. The bulk of the existence that you are living is not real existence but rather an existence fabricated by your mind.

Let me give you an example. It may first seem revolting to you, but it shows the power of the mind in a blunt and striking way.

One day Swâmiji reminded me to what extent we are prisoners of
our limited desires and of our refusals. This is particularly true in
the domain of our likes and dislikes of certain foods, for it is none
other than the mind that decrees to one person that he cannot eat
cheese and to another that he cannot eat peach fuzz. I was led to
give him the example of how one day, as a small child, I ate my
own excrement; this very much surprised my mother. "But,"
Swâmiji told me, "many little children do that without feeling the
slightest disgust." As I knew I had done so myself, I remained
neutral to these words. Then he added: "Consequently today, if
you are free from the mind, you can very well eat a little of your
own stool." I felt myself immediately shrink back inside, and
realized to what extent I refused such a proposal. And yet . . . and
yet . . . Since at the age of one and a half, in my playpen, I, Arnaud,
was caught by my mother with my mouth full—since I found it fine
at the time and did not die of it—why was it impossible for the same
Arnaud, at the age of forty-five, to put his own excrement into his
mouth? There you see the absolute power of the mind—stronger
than any decision I could make. Yet even such a refusal could be
turned into acceptance, if put into a vast understanding of the whole.
We know that certain Tibetans indulge, at least once, in acts equally
repulsive in order to surpass the labels of the mind.

Swâmiji concluded: "In the same way, your entire existence
is controlled by the mind. You live in an all-powerful world created by the mind." And after that, we talk of Liberation! And even
of destroying the mind, without having the slightest idea of what
those words imply!

Our existence is the exact destiny that corresponds to us. If
we learn to appreciate everything it brings us, day after day, then
we will become capable of acting. The best way to destroy the mind
is to experience the two aspects of reality. *Upa-bhoga* will never
destroy the mind—on the contrary. But *bhoga*, real appreciation, will
little by little awaken you to the real world—the objective world.
This is no small matter. It will take a long time to learn to appreciate painful situations. And it will take a long time to learn to savor
happy ones—without feeling divided and uneasy, and without
unconscious ulterior motives. You will then become a doer, no

longer simply a machine that reacts. You will awaken and escape
from your world, to live in *the* world.

As for the word *jnani*, it means "knowledge." Depending on
the prefix added to the word, the type of knowledge varies. *Jnani*
means Knowledge which is a function of being. In English, you
distinguish between *"to know"* and *"to know about."* If you know
how to swim, you know swimming. If you have read twelve books
on all kinds of swimming, you know a lot about swimming, but
you do not know swimming. A theologian *knows about God*; a mystic
knows God. Unfortunately, we confuse true knowledge, which is
real experience, with learning. We know much about many things,
but we do not really know those things.

You can accumulate information on wisdom and on yoga, yet
be neither a sage nor a yogi. I wrote *Ashrams*, a book which I am
still ready to recommend to you today, but 95% of that book spoke
of things I did not know. I knew much about wisdom because I
had been interested in it for twelve years and had consulted swâmis
and gurus. But I did not really know what I wrote in that book.

We are all subject to this confusion between real knowledge,
which is part of our being, and erudition. You can write a book on
swimming without being able to do a lap of the breast-stroke. Only
karta, the doer, and *bhokta*, the appreciator of both the pleasant and
the unpleasant faces of existence, can become *jnani*, one who has
true knowledge. You can be a Don Juan, and still die without ever
knowing the secret of sex—if you lack a complete, deep, conscious,
total experience of the *whole* of existence.

***

With *maha karta, maha bhokta* and *maha jnani*, we change planes
and enter straight onto the level of what is called Awakening,
Wisdom, Liberation. Only one who has become *karta*—therefore,
someone who is a doer—can surpass this stage. By developing
consciousness of being, he can discover that he is actually not the
doer of his actions. He has attained the *egoless state*. The most famous
Christian description of this is by St. Paul: "I no longer live as I

myself, but Christ lives within me." I no longer act as I myself, but Christ acts within me; I no longer appreciate suffering or joy as I myself, but Christ appreciates them within me; I no longer know as I myself, but Christ knows within me.

Once you are no longer an accumulation of anarchistic tendencies, like a parliament whose members argue among themselves; once you have become, instead, like a kingdom formed around a sovereign, a real doer, a real appreciator and a real knower, then the little individualized ego can transcend the feeling of being separated and discover that "I no longer live as I myself." Then "I"—with my qualifications, my limitations, my tastes, my distastes, my particular way of liking what I like, and of not liking what I dislike—this "I" will have disappeared. You become the Great Appreciator, *maha bhokta*. There is a full and entire appreciation of all situations—from the most "terrible" to the most "marvelous." You become the Great Doer, sometimes also called the non-doer. You also become *maha jnani*, the supreme Knower whose Knowledge is no longer relative but instead absolute, transcending time, separation, division, multiplicity, attraction and repulsion. This is the goal of all spiritual teachings. Once the sense of ego is effaced, I no longer live as I myself, but *Atma Shakti* lives within me.

How does one attain this state? What is the way for you? While waiting for supreme Knowledge, center your existence on the three words: *karta*, *bhokta* and *jnani*. A certain type of Hinduism did me wrong by immediately presenting the word *karta* as a notion to be surpassed, and the word *bhoga* as attachment to the world of the senses—a world which you must renounce in order to discover the Absolute. *Upa-bhoga*—false, impulsive and mechanical appreciation— will always keep you in ignorance. You will never be *jnani*, he who knows; you will always be *ajnani*, the unknowing one. At ninety years of age, life will have taught you nearly nothing. Only complete knowing changes your being.

Center your life on these three words and never let yourself be troubled by what you may read in books on Hinduism. To whom was the translated phrase addressed? To whom was the sage speaking? In what context? It was not to you that he said those words. In Jean Herbert's translation of *The Teachings of Mâ*

Anandamayî, the word *bhoga* is condemned many times. Replace it each time with *upa-bhoga.* And remember that *bhoga* does not merely mean profane enjoyment. It means the real experience of each moment of existence. This is possible for you. However, you will only become the Great Doer, the Great Appreciator, the Great Sage, if you first wholeheartedly become a doer, an appreciator and a knower.

"To know is to be." You see—it is a concrete program. With that single phrase from the Yoga Vashishtha, Swâmiji showed me the totality of the Way he was offering. At first, I only partly understood, because the mind, old habits and encrusted errors were too strong. But little by little, those words took on meaning. Then I realized to what extent I had originally deluded myself. I had asked the impossible of myself, after reading Hindu texts that were too advanced for me. And I realized that I was not a doer because I had never been an appreciator.

I often refer to the Gurdjieff Teachings. I do not deny that those teachings saved me at the age of twenty-four, when I was completely lost. They gave me something to hold onto, yet I cannot say I learned a great deal. Nonetheless, today I would reproach the way I personally received those Teachings. This has nothing to do with Gurdjieff himself—a man I never met during his lifetime. I strived hard to become *karta,* a doer. If I am self-aware, I can "do." If I am identified, and have lost "self awareness," my actions are mechanical reactions. I trained myself in self-awareness, in feeling as described in Hinayana Buddhist manuals: "When the disciple inhales, he knows: 'I am inhaling deeply'; when the disciple exhales, he knows: 'I am exhaling deeply.' " This I practiced to the point of no longer acting naturally. I opened doors slowly and consciously, turned my head slowly, and talked in a measured voice in order to be really aware, and not to let myself re-identify with the stream of conversation. Yet I had not understood the secret I am sharing with you—that you can only be a real doer if you are an appreciator of the "bad" as well as the "good." In fact, if you read between the lines, this is suggested in the book *In Search of the Miraculous,* but in actual practice, it had escaped me. Yet an understanding of the meaning which Swâmiji gave to the words *bhoga,* "appreciation," and *bhokta*, "the appreciator," is something that escapes the majority of men and women I used to know, fellow travelers who visited India's ashrams in quest of Realization. Remember, *bhoga* means the complete appreciation of the unpleasant as well as the pleasant, and it is only this non-dualistic experience which brings you knowledge. Otherwise, you will never know what is to be known, and you will die as blind and as ignorant as you were born . . . no matter what efforts you make to act more consciously.

***

A very famous, but simple, saying by Buddha declares: "Suffering is being joined to that which we do not like; suffering is being separated from that which we like." In two sentences, Buddha described the human condition. And he declared that it was possible to free oneself from suffering. The different Hinayana and Mahayana schools tried to outdo him in philosophical debates; however, Buddha just put aside all the metaphysical arguments which were bogging down the Hinduism of his time. All of Buddhism is contained in what are called "the four noble truths." First, there is suffering. And what is suffering? Being separated from what we like is suffering; being joined to what we do not like is suffering. Second, it is possible to escape suffering. Third, there is a cause for suffering—slavery to this mechanism. Fourth, there is a way to escape this mechanism.

Following the path Buddha pointed out means that being tied to what we do not like will no longer be suffering, and being separated from what we like, will no longer be suffering. It seems impossible, yet if indeed there is a way out, this can only be it. Any Way based on the fundamental opposition between what we like and what we do not like, any attempt to make what we like in our lives, triumph over what we do not like . . . is a false, deceptive, useless path that leads nowhere.

The only real Way is to overcome the feeling that: "what is fortunate is fortunate, and what is unfortunate is unfortunate." This is the basis on which all men's lives are founded. Each of us func-

Lust

tions according to his unconscious, his nature, his deep tendencies. As long as you do not admit that this is precisely what must be overcome, you can practice zazen for an hour every morning (which shows definite will power and decisiveness), and you can go to India every year, but you will not escape the ego, and you will never find the deep peace and inner freedom which you were promised.

This Way is open before you at every moment. To consciously appreciate each minute that you live, or not to do so . . . "that is the question." Being "identified" when you are enjoying a situation is what is called avidity, *lust*. You are not consciously there in yourself to satisfy your desires. It is your desires that satisfy themselves at your expense. That should be clear for you. Lust does not indicate an action, but rather the manner of accomplishing it. There is a greedy, selfish manner which is actually lust, even if you are making love with your own spouse; and there is a conscious, free manner to taste life, because you accept the two aspects of existence. What has above been called lust, is simply the expression of the ordinary attitude: "I want the happy side; I refuse the painful side." But one who, even while living a happy moment, is ready deep inside to also accept whatever suffering may come, such a person can live that happy moment without lust.

Do not see any rejection in the words "sacrifice" and "renouncement." See them rather as a call to no longer cling, to no longer be attached, to no longer be tense. If I hold a precious object in my hand, I must not hold it in a tightened fist, but rather in an open hand. As truly religious people say—be they Christians or Moslems—"God gives, and God takes away." But no one asks you to reject what God has not taken away. You may end up mutilating yourself in the name of some kind of spiritual ideal, and further increase your inner confusion. Take and receive. Take and receive without lust. I accept with my whole heart what is pleasant; I accept with my whole heart what is unpleasant. Then I am free to act.

Blessed be the day when you hear this resolution vibrate within you for the first time: "I can no longer stand to be a fool who learns nothing from life. It is unworthy of me. I want to be one who has knowledge—therefore I must also appreciate the negative pole of existence. Quick, let me suffer so I can at last live it consciously, taste it fully, savor it, and be free from it. I am tied to what I do not like; I am cut off from what I like. This is the suffering aspect of total existence, and I am going to acquire the real experience of it—*bhoga.*"

Suffering takes on a different meaning. It becomes our best opportunity to attain Liberation during this lifetime. That is why Christians say that God sends trials to those He loves, to bring them closer to Him. This sounds morbid to those who understand nothing about spirituality. Suffering is a support. You take support on the ground to walk, you take support on water to swim, and you take support on the experience of reality in order to progress. Suffering is a great opportunity. Do not let it escape you any more. Afterwards, if you wish, you can act to eliminate the cause. On the one hand, say "yes" with all your being, and on the other, take whatever measures and make whatever decisions are possible.

What is it that keeps you in illusion, in error, in blindness? The fact that, although it is the right thing to do, you do not want to appreciate the painful aspect of existence. This refusal is fundamental to you. It is rooted inside you, but you are eliminating half of existence. Therefore you are letting the chance to progress escape you. You still think that spirituality is going to make the painful aspect disappear, and the happy aspect predominate. You think that by some miracle, you will succeed in everything. No. Socrates did not succeed in everything—he was condemned to drink hemlock. Jesus Christ did not succeed in everything—he was crucified. Ramana Maharshi did not succeed in everything—he died of cancer. Mâ Anandamayî did not succeed in everything—in spite of herself, she was involved in a financial scandal over the construction of a "Mâ Anandamayî Hospital" beside her ashram at Benares. Even Mâ Anandamayî was subjected to what would be for you a source of worry and sleepless nights. But she was the most sublime manifestation that I ever came upon, not only of *maha jnani* "the great Sage," and of *maha karta* "the great Doer," but also of *maha bhokta* "the great Appreciator." One had only to see the way she lived.

It is an entirely false idea that the Sage—who has died to himself

and to the world, and is totally turned toward the Center—
has become insensitive to the manifest world. The Sage has truly
become the Great Appreciator. But you can have no idea of such
total, impersonal, beyond-the-ego appreciation, as long as your
deep-seated opposition between what is "good" and "bad" has
not been overcome at the source. Everything works toward the
good of those who love God. Never again say "that's terrible."
Never again. No matter what happens, say: that is very interesting . . . that will help me to understand, to know and to progress.
And do not let one single opportunity escape you ever again.

3

MAN'S THREE BRAINS

If you wish to know yourself and understand how you function, certain outlines will be necessary—ones which apply to all human beings, men or women—for within these outlines, you will find your own personal expressions. You know of the Hindu distinction of three bodies, for example (the physical, the subtle and the causal) or of the five *koshas*, five levels of increasingly subtle functioning (physical, physiological, psychological, logical and mystical). If you do not let yourself be thrown off by names which at first seem unpronounceable—such as *manomayakosha* or *vijnan-amayakosha*—this is a simple, complete, rich classification, whereas the descriptions given in modern books on psychology are often extremely complicated.

Swâmiji also used three words which are quite easy to understand: *physical, emotional* and *mental*. This distinction was immediately familiar to me because it reminded me of one I had already read at the age of twenty-four; it was in a book by Ouspensky which I often quote, named *In Search of the Miraculous*, on the teachings of Gurdjieff. The years pass. Gurdjieff gave those teachings to Ouspensky in 1917-1918. The book was published in 1949, but the truths themselves never go out of fashion.

This classification of human functioning into three categories (physical, emotional and mental—or intellectual) is practically universal among traditional teachings. Yet we are sometimes plunged into confusion by the vocabulary used. This is particularly true when it is a case of ancient Greek or Latin translations (or even more so when it concerns Arabic, Hebrew or Sanskrit) and when other words arise, ones which we do not often situate very clearly . . . like soul, spirit, volitions, apperceptions, drives and affects. A simple diagram is necessary. Actually, there is no ordinary human activity (apart from meditation or higher states of consciousness) which does not enter into one of these functions. In the book *In Search of the Miraculous*, Gurdjieff called these functions "centers."

It is interesting to note that in his difficult and arduous book *Beelzebub's Tales to His Grandson* (one which many people have purchased but only very few have read), Gurdjieff employs the word "brain" instead of the word "center," and describes the human being as a "three-brained being." It is an expression proper to Gurdjieff, and one which comes up frequently throughout the book. Old Beelzebub (long exiled to the solar system, one of the most unpleasant parts of the entire universe) answers his grandson's questions and speaks to him of the "strange functionings of the three-brained beings who populate the planet Earth." The expression "three-brained beings" was mocked by superficial readers or badly-informed listeners. Yet it is an important one to reflect upon. I must admit that even while I was struggling to read *Beelzebub's Tales to His Grandson*, when my "search" was centered on the Gurdjieff groups, I did not fully grasp the value of that expression. It was only little by little, with Swâmiji, when I was able to concretely put the teaching of truth into practice, that the wealth of that strange appellation appeared to me.

Just what does the word "center" or "brain" signify, since it does not only mean the brain found within the skull? Put modern science aside for the moment. In a specific sense, that which we call a "brain" is a function which both receives information and decides on a response. This takes place by means of a double movement from the outside toward the inside, and from the inside toward the outside. In this sense, the word "brain" can be used for much other than grey matter. Any slightly elaborate device—robot or computer—capable of receiving, processing and responding to information, is thereby a "brain."

I wish to emphasize that there is a double movement: from the outside in and from the inside out. This is particularly clear as far as our intellectual center is concerned: we gather a certain amount of data, reflect on it, and either *react* mechanically or *respond* consciously. When you write, the response passes through your body, through your hand. When you speak, it also comes through your body, through the larynx, vocal cords and mouth. However you could also keep this response for yourself, in which case it would not leave your brain: "Let's see, there is a given amount of

internal MAP of reality

money available: a certain sum is necessary per square yard, there are a given number of square yards, so here is the total cost. Can I borrow . . . at what rate . . . on what terms of repayment?"

Information comes to us from outside: we receive, assimilate, assess and compare it. Reflecting and reasoning, we use the training and instruction we have received; through a method, through our skill for solving problems of one sort or another, we come up with a response (one which is perhaps excellent, perhaps deplorable—that is another question!). A very intelligent man can thus be termed "a great brain" or "a mastermind." Wide ranging minds are needed everywhere: in politics, business, science. But this intellectual function, or mental level, does not compose a total human being.

Although I do not wish to further explore this theme today, let us first look at the sexual center—a center which also has its own intelligence and can function as a fourth brain. From the duality point of view, as soon as one feels incomplete and looks for a complement outside oneself, there is sexuality. This is very often the meaning of the words of the ancient Yogic or Upanishadic texts. Any attempt to relate with someone other than oneself is therefore considered sexuality. We can acknowledge sexuality as Freud described it as already starting at infancy. But normal sexual function appears at puberty when the male, consciously, seeks to mate with the female, and the female, consciously, seeks to mate with the male. In this restricted sense, the sexual center can also be considered as a "brain." The information received is: "this woman is beautiful, attractive and desirable," and the response, in its raw state, is: "I want to mate with her," either without further ado or after a courtship display. We function first of all in an animal-like way . . . more or less educated (or more often trained) by the circumstances of human life in society.

From the purely physiological aspect, this response is an erection for a man and the secretion of the glands which moisten the vagina for a woman. But today I will go no further along that line since the sexual function, in this limited sense, does not appear at the very beginning of life. Having appeared after the others, it disappears before them. Generally, after a certain age, this mating function is no longer found—at least in normal human beings. However, we will now study two other centers which function as "brains": the physical center and the emotional center.

The book *In Search of the Miraculous* divides the physical center into two parts. It is a very simple distinction. This center is at times considered in itself, and at others, in its two subdivisions: instinctive and motor. "Instinctive" covers all which does not need to be learned; "motor" concerns that which needs to be taught and learned. A baby does not learn to nurse. Imagine a baby with limp lips at its mother's breast, not taking in its mother's milk--it would have to be fed by tube or some other artificial method. But from the very first time it nurses at its mother's breast, the baby *knows*. This is unmistakably instinctive behavior. Instinctive behavior also includes all physiological functioning over which we ordinarily have no control. Hatha yoga breathing exercises can be taught, but a baby is not taught to breathe. A child can be shown the finger movements for the piano or the guitar, but he does not learn the heart movements, the contractions which drive the blood into the arteries, nor the secretion of the endocrine glands. In the heart there is a "brain" . . . the wisdom of the body . . . homeostasis . . . the extremely complex way in which exterior information is treated by this instinctive center, which responds by contracting or dilating certain vessels, secreting adrenaline or endorphines and so forth. Even if you have never taken an interest in natural sciences, you can see an "intelligence" at work, taking the appropriate measures. This is how we resist illness and secrete antibodies. A large part of medical studies is centered on this aspect of the instinctive physical level, one which needs neither to be taught nor to be learned.

But the "motor" center must be educated. If children were not taught to walk, they would stay on all fours. I have read that young birds would not know by themselves how to fly unless their parents taught them. Our motor center can be more or less educated, more or less perfected. We also have a small possibility of educating our instinctive center; at least one of those functions which normally escapes our control can be dominated. This, as you know, is breathing. Although it is very interesting in itself, we will not go into this possibility of intervening in the instinctive functions, starting with a voluntary, deliberate intervention in the breathing function.

In its motor aspect, the physical center must be entirely educated. We have learned everything—otherwise we would only be capable of a few extremely awkward gestures, consisting uniquely in grasping and destroying. The body, this particular brain, very quickly learns to directly treat information without passing through the intellectual brain. Part of what is found in the cranium does indeed intervene, but we are not speaking of the organs, but rather of the function. Tradition does not locate this function in the head, but rather in the lower abdomen—where the *hara* is situated— and in the spinal column. In fact the entire body is involved, processing and responding to the information. In a game of Ping-Pong, where the time for reaction is extremely brief, if it were up to the head to decide how to return the opponent's ball, imagine the result! When you return a ball in table tennis, the information is perceived (how and where the ball arrives), and a response is furnished (how will you return the ball . . . forehand, backhand, turning the wrist just so, and applying a certain force in order to place the ball exactly where you want it). This is what makes a real player, one who wants to win points against his opponent. To do so, there must have been education; every champion must once have played for the first time.

It is the intelligence of this motor center which is educated. The body is not simply a conglomeration of relatively agile or well-developed muscles, enabling one to lift more or less heavy weights. The instinctive center has an intelligence and the motor center has an intelligence. Indeed, we must admit that each individual is more or less gifted—and this is true for all functionings. Those who are very gifted learn more quickly, or sometimes they hardly even need to learn; those who are less gifted must work, study and practice much more. But the motor center is obviously a "brain" in the sense that it receives information, makes a decision and responds to the information. The intellectual brain intervenes at the beginning of this education: "Wait, explain this to me. You say I have a tendency to bend my wrist when it should be straight, and to lift my elbow; so should I lower my elbow? Oh I see, I am holding the paddle in the wrong way—all right." It is the same when you start to learn where to put your fingers on a keyboard, or where to put your feet on the pedals of a car. Then comes a time when your head no longer intervenes. You find that you are able to drive—letting the clutch in and out and downshifting, all without even realizing it. And while driving you can even carry on a difficult conversation.

The physical center therefore directly processes information and directly decides on a response—more or less intelligently, in relation to how gifted or educated it is—without passing through the head. This is an important point to understand because what is called "vigilance," "self-remembering," "consciousness" or *"awareness"* is something other than actual intellectual functioning. Vigilance is definitely not the interference of the head in sexual, bodily and emotional functionings. The body is a brain sufficient in itself, it can function either without vigilance and completely identified in a situation, or with vigilance and aware. For example, you can drive while distracted, without being conscious that "you are" and that you are driving . . . without awareness, without self-remembering (which is the way to Self-remembering), and without vigilance (which is one of the common factors of all spiritual teachings without exception, be they religious or metaphysical, dualistic or non-dualistic). You can drive, stop at a red light, start up on the green light, and put on the turn signal . . . all in "sleep." Or else you can be vigilant.

But being vigilant, being aware, does not mean making the head once again intervene in a motor function, as it did when you started learning a skill. Vigilance is like a light that turns on. You can function without the light of vigilance burning, or you can function with it. You can be in a state of meditation while driving, or you can drive without the slightest inkling of awareness.

The intelligence of the body can hence be more or less developed. This is by no means an original statement. But we live in a modern society which gives an abnormal, unbalanced and unharmonious predominance to the intelligence of the head. This is easy to see. Even tests for employment or professional orientation appeal essentially to the head.

Indeed, in many activities where book learning plays only a limited role, recruiting is now done according to the level of studies. ("Yes, we realize that it will be of no use later, but after all, there has to be some way of selecting people.")

I am asking you to escape this modern deformation and to understand that man, as Gurdjieff said, is a three-brained being (who also has a distinct sexual brain), and that the intelligence of the body can be developed to a large extent. This latter is the body's capacity to process information directly and to work out a response, not just in table tennis, but in all of life's circumstances. Some slip and fall; others slip and know how to regain their balance. This intelligence of the body intervenes in all physical activities. Educating the motor function is not just increasing muscular strength or agility, it is educating one's "intelligence."

As for the intellectual function—to what extent do studies really fulfill this function? To what extent does the intellect become more apt to receive exterior information well, to assimilate and compare it, to perform certain work on it and to give a response? A head which works well is not the same as one which is brimful. Although these functions are actually linked and have certain repercussions on each other, just for a moment imagine this brain functioning independently. It sometimes works quite well; it is this intellectual function which is responsible for technological exploits, well-made decisions and rapid solutions to problems.

But all too often, the intellectual brain starts to ramble—either because it has badly received outside information, or because it processes the information badly and therefore furnishes an inappropriate response. It is clear that if you must take ten parameters into account, and you only consider five of them, then you have cut off outside information. It is the same thing if you deform information (if you curve what is straight, straighten what is curved, enlarge what is small, or decrease what is large). It is important to educate this center—not by memorizing more and more facts, but rather by learning to correct these distortions and to *see* reality as it is, from day to day, without letting projections from your unconscious or arbitrary choices deform your reception of information. With false information, you cannot find a right response. Re-education is first of all necessary on that point.

Where is my intelligence of the head lacking, aside from any question of scholarliness or exams? One can be a sage without being a doctor of philosophy, believe me. Ramana Maharshi and Mâ Anandamayî never went to college. You must do long work to become conscious of the fact that your intellectual center functions badly, and of how deformed your perceptions and conceptions are. You do not see people and situations as they are, or you only do in those instances when you yourself are in no way concerned or put into question (for example when you are solving a problem concerning the strength of materials and the type of steel girder to use). Most often you are personally involved; therefore, you are not objective. Rather than functioning through intelligence (*buddhi*), the brain receives information incorrectly colored by "mind."

Moreover, the head can function badly while processing information—and therefore in choosing a response. In different areas of life, it can arrive at conclusions which later, in practice, turn out either to be disastrous or, in any case, worse than a different solution. It is the brain which decides: "Considering the present economic situation, I am selling property I inherited" or "I will not sell it", "I will sell it when the repairs are finished,"or"I am going to sell it in its present state, without finishing the repairs." But "what does the situation merit?"

Now, current thinking tends to believe that this processing of information is most important in order to educate the intellectual center. Yes, that is true—it is important. But how is it that human beings are so often wrong outside the realm of pure technology? It is admirable to send men to the moon and bring them back to earth again, but I am speaking about your personal lives and of areas other than pure technology, politics, economics and business management. Why is it that the result which, so to speak, comes out of this intellectual center is inappropriate? The fault is not essentially due to bad treatment of information, but rather to bad reception of information . . . and that is what is too often forgotten.

You think you have correctly understood the facts of a situation—but you have not given the right response. So you decide to reflect, compare, elaborate and come to a better decision. Yet I insist on the fact that there is a much more important and considerably neglected area to be considered: improving your reception of the information. If we conduct ourselves unintelligently in life, it is because we are processing information which is not the real information. There is a deformation in our very reception of the facts. "Intelligent" people make mistakes because their brains are not capable of providing them with the real and complete facts, and giving the right weight to those facts.

***

Finally there is a third brain—the heart center—which the book *In Search of the Miraculous* calls the emotional center. But its emotions, as I have so often said, are destined to disappear. "I am unhappy, " "I am happy," "it is so beautiful," "it is overwhelming," "it is terrible," "it is atrocious," "it is shameful," "it is sublime"—all are typical expressions of emotional language. This emotional center is also to be seen as a brain which can function independently of the head, thereby receiving information, processing it, and providing a response. Yet as a "brain"—and therefore as an intelligence—the emotional center in most human beings functions deplorably.

The intellectual training we have received must be taken for what it is. It nonetheless produces men capable of holding an important position for twenty years without having to be put aside—men who put forth undeniably positive results. The physical training we have received allows us to skillfully handle our fork and spoon, drive a car or perhaps even become tennis champions or circus acrobats. But the training our emotional center has received, the training of the heart as a "brain," is practically non-existent.

In past times, a child received this education from his family background, group and social class. Such was the case in all societies, not only in India. And the primary function of religion (of Islam, Buddhism and Hinduism as well as Christianity) was to educate this intelligence of the heart. This intelligence of feeling was not considered as an incoherent collection of "I like—I don't like," but rather as an instrument indispensable for our existence if we were to be worthy of the name "man". Any religion which has not degenerated teaches the heart to perceive and appreciate existential facts, to situate them in the whole, to process them and to decide on a response just as a brain does. We are three-brained beings, but predominance is given to our I.Q. and our capacity to pass exams. And tests give but little indication—very little indeed—of the level of development of this intelligence of the heart.

***

If you want to progress (even without taking account of ultimate, metaphysical realities and instead remaining within duality and the habitual consciousness of the self), you can only do so if you are convinced of your nature as a three-brained being. The three centers have equal importance. Yet you cannot admit this fact: "No, I will never believe that the motor center is as important as the intellectual one. The motor center can make you into a great champion or an acrobat, but it is not because of the motor center that we managed to send men to the moon." This is definitely so, but the life of a human being does not solely consist in working as a NASA engineer.

A Yogi in the larger sense of the term, committed to the Way of Liberation, does much more work on the body than on the intellect. Once he has read Patanjali's Yoga Sutras (not to be able to endlessly comment on them, but to have access to a summarized memorandum), everything else takes place between himself and his master. He does not live bent over books to underline and note, in order to get a bachelor's, master's or doctorate degree.

All human beings do not achieve the fullness of human possibilities. This is also true. A person can be gifted in one of these centers more so than in another. But, on principle, stop favoring the intelligence of the head and forgetting the intelligence of the body—as we all do, or have done in the past. Too often, one does not reflect on the "brain" aspect of these functions; the body's intelligence is taken for a skill which is acquired once and for all, a specialty. Once he has learned his trade well, a ladies' hairdresser has the trade in his fingers; he does good permanents and cuts. A man who has certain manual or motor capacities is valued only as one who has "learned" something and knows it physically. No matter how many hair-styling or tennis lessons you may have taken, you will only be a good tennis player or a good hairdresser if you have a motor center which functions as a "brain," *feeling* the information, processing it and responding. You forget the "intelligence" aspect of the body, which is independent of the head and capable of "thinking" and "deciding" (with the slight difference that the body's function of thought and decision is several thousand times faster than that of the head). In tai chi, karate and the Japanese martial arts, observe the speed with which the body receives information on the opponent's moves, or even his intention, and immediately decides on the response. As for the responses of the instinctive center, they are even faster.

How long does it take a dose of potassium cyanide to cause death? There are so many complex procedures which our instinctive physical functioning is capable of accomplishing in a fraction of a second!

Each center always functions as a brain. There is a movement from the outside toward the inside in order to receive information, and a movement from the inside toward the outside to furnish a response—or what would perhaps commonly be called a reaction. But in this teaching, we carefully distinguish between reaction and action. Or action is sometimes designated by the term "response," implying an element of consciousness which is not found in reaction. A robot can react marvelously, but it will never be able to increase its consciousness of the self.

As far as the brain of the heart is concerned, the situation is particularly deplorable because of the constant predominance given to the brain of the intellect. Understand that you no longer have the right to consider yourself intelligent—even with your doctorate—if your intelligence of the heart is nonexistent. No human being can consider himself highly developed if he keeps a stupid heart. Unfortunately, some intellectually or physically brilliant human beings have a stupid heart. I am asking you today to consider this function of feeling as an "intelligence."

The body can perceive sensations of cold, of warmth, and so forth. The head can perceive relations of cause and effect, but only on an intellectual level. Certain elements of reality can only be received or perceived by the heart—in particular the emotions of others, which play an immense role in our existences. We lead a communal life with directors, employees, colleagues, associates, clients, retailers, uncles, aunts, brothers-in-law, parents, sons, daughters, wives and perhaps lovers and mistresses. And these human beings, with whom so many different types of relationships are established, all have emotions. Our motor intelligence only allows us to perceive these emotions in a very imperfect manner; as for our head, it cannot *understand* but can only *qualify*—"You definitely seem nervous today"—without even knowing why, what is the matter, and what is the truth of that emotion. Only the heart, if it functions well, can receive these elements which are indispensable to a right and successful life within a network of relationships. This is a factor which we should always take into account in order to avoid elementary behavior which merits no more than the name reaction—and indeed reaction inappropriate to the near or distant goal towards which we are striving.

This may all be new for you if you have not looked at things in this light. Man is a three-brained being; the third brain is the heart. (I prefer to say the heart, rather than the emotional center, because the emotions are indeed destined to disappear.) Only a well-functioning, purified heart can enable us to understand the emotions of others and subsequently to take into consideration these emotions which are the center of their lives, fears, desires, worries, hopes, sufferings, and projections of the unconscious. It is the intelligence of the heart which is the intelligence of sages.

But until now, the heart has been everything but an instrument of knowledge and an intelligence; instead it is cluttered with joys, sorrows, fits of enthusiasm, dreams, divine moments, despair, discouragement and suicidal impulses. How much work must yet be done for the heart to learn to receive the information it is to process! Understanding is of primary importance; processing the information comes afterwards. But there are responses which only the heart can provide. No matter how knowledgeable you may be in psychology, psychoanalysis and psychotherapy, there are responses that the head can never give—or unfortunately, it will give responses but they will be inappropriate. It is the heart which decides, after processing the information, that: "there will be a smile," "there will be a severe look," "there will be gentle, consoling words," "there will be firm words or perhaps the roar of a Zen master." Only the heart is entitled to make that sort of decision. The heart is the most highly-perfected instrument of a human being, yet in actual fact it is the one which is the most dilapidated and the most badly used.

Feeling gives us very precise information on a whole aspect of reality to which the head has no access. Of course, if it is a question of writing a letter, the "response" can come through the head and the body—since you use your hand to hold the pen. But the head and the body have become only instruments. The directing organ, the control center, is the heart. How can you expect to be a control center if you do not receive the information which enables you to control? You have an emotional brain which you do not use—or which you use very little—because it functions badly and you have not learned how to handle it. That is why it is so important to purify the heart and to let the emotions fade away.

Your self-esteem, your pride, your dignity must lead you to feel what an intolerable failing it is for you, a human being, to maintain a heart cluttered with emotions. Your intelligence has very little value if you lack this intelligence of the heart. What is essential to feeling, in its role as a brain, is perceiving information well, no longer deforming it. But emotion deforms, emotion distorts—whether it be repulsion (called a "negative" emotion) or even fascination, dazzling and blinding us to all other elements of a situation.

So when one of your three brains functions so badly that it is practically in a "coma" or in indescribable disorder, how can you be surprised that your existence does not unfold as you wish it would? You seek true love and marital happiness, yet you are divorcing for the fifth time, though you have always dreamed only of fidelity. You would like to make friendship and love reign in the world because you have idealistic ideas, yet you are on bad terms with several people. And more complex examples abound. But you cannot hope for a successful existence if the brain of the heart does not function. You cannot imagine solving certain intellectual problems if you are mentally deficient, and still you accept being emotionally deficient.

However you manage to delude yourself, because you are perhaps quite gifted on the motor level, being very good at skiing or in some other sport. Or you may be brilliant on the intellectual level, easily passing all exams. The situation is serious when even an apprentice-carpenter spends a good part of his carpentry studies wielding pens, notebooks, books and courses. In the past we knew that true intelligence of the body meant directly perceiving information (the strength and grain of the wood) and providing a response (the best way to use that wood). But, like an intellectual, even the most skillful craftsman can also be emotionally deficient.

Until now, perhaps you have considered the heart, the seat of emotions, especially in terms of your suffering or your happiness. You have been more or less unhappy, more or less happy, more or less often unhappy, more or less often happy. And now you hope that psychotherapy, asceticism, or a spiritual practice can put some order into your emotional world, to make you more happy and more often happy. But you have not sufficiently regarded it in terms of intelligence and stupidity, rather than simply in terms of happiness and unhappiness. The real Way, no longer a preparatory way, begins when you have understood with your whole being that the heart is an instrument of knowledge and decision, that a large part of the knowledge which comes to you is knowledge deformed by emotions and that most decisions made by the heart are idiotic decisions. We do not perceive anything of the emotions, sufferings, and hopes of our own son or daughter, wife or husband, or of those who direct us, who collaborate with us or work for us.

***

But there is more. This intelligence of the heart does more than process information dealing with the emotional aspect of situations. Feeling, as an instrument of knowledge in its place between the physical brain and the intellectual brain, also perceives the whole of reality. The only way I can only relate to the tape recorder here in front of me is through touch; it immediately tells me—without my having to think—that the object has a certain form, occupies a certain volume in space, and is composed of certain materials. Then the head tells me: it is an instrument of magnetic sound recording and not one that cuts records.

And, the brain of the heart which is so important . . . what does it tell you about the tape recorder? Ah, unfortunately, it tells modern man nothing—unless it be to arouse an emotion (I like it or I don't like it) and a few unconscious projections. These will depend on whether the tape recorder itself is associated with nice memories for you—perhaps it was your father who offered you your first one, when you were a child—or whether, on the other hand, it is associated with bad memories because you once had to study recorded lessons which did not interest you in the least. This emotional memory gives you no real information.

The heart should be an instrument of knowledge, always and in all situations. There should be an embryonic development going on—to which you should attach great importance—enabling your heart to participate in your life truthfully, intelligently and without distortion. How can you become a complete and harmonious being, with all the functions nature has given you as a human being at your disposal, to help you pursue your quest and discover ultimate Consciousness? You accept having an invalid heart much more easily than one who is infirm, stricken with chronic progressive polyarthritis at the age of seventeen, accepts being bedridden.

"That is beautiful" means "I find that beautiful." It is not true knowledge. Knowledge is objective, not subjective. When I say that the heart is an instrument of knowledge, I mean exact knowledge. The heart as an instrument of knowledge functions in the same manner for all sages. Remember the words of Heraclitus: "Those who have awakened all live in the same world, but those who are still sleeping each live in a different world." Except on some still hypothetical data, all physicists—be they Catholics, homosexuals, freemasons, Communists, Russians or Americans—all of them agree. As for knowledge of the heart, if it is real knowledge then we should all be speaking the same language. But this fact no longer means anything to virtually any modern Westerners.

We used to sit on a little folded blanket across from Swâmiji. One day, at the end of my talk with him, I threw the blanket over to its place rather than placing it there carefully. Swâmiji said to me: "How did you treat that blanket? During all our talks these last few days, it has allowed you to be more comfortably seated to ask questions and to listen to the responses. It has contributed to helping you along the way, in your quest for that which is most important. And how did that blanket come to the ashram to help you take better advantage of your talks with Swâmiji? Have you thought with gratitude of the farm laborers who cultivated the cotton in the torrid heat of India . . . of those who picked, spun, dyed and wove it . . . of the merchants who organized its collection, transport and distribution in the selling places?" And while Swâmiji was speaking, in Swâmiji's presence, under Swâmiji's gaze . . . feeling awakened in me. My heart revealed much to me about that blanket, much that my head could not tell me—much that even the sense of touch could tell me, for it was decidedly more comfortable than sitting on the cement.

There is not a single element of relative reality which cannot also be perceived through the heart. True knowledge of anything (a fact, an object, a person, a situation, a "here and now") is knowledge provided by the three brains simultaneously. There can only be true comprehension as long as the three brains function together. You cannot know anything just from touch and what the intellect tells you about it. The feeling center is the only one capable of perceiving certain information, and the only one capable of providing certain responses.

***

So many of the questions I am asked show how much the head predominates for you. Parents ask me intellectual questions about child raising—as if the answers were to be found in books by Doctor

Spock. But it is only the heart that can give you the information which is essential for raising your children. And it is only the heart that can make the decisions. It is the intelligence of the heart that can tell you if you should scold, smile, give in or refuse, if you should insist on yogurt or if you should let the child never touch yogurt. Never will the head alone give you the answers in this area. You forget that the heart is an intelligence and you try to be educators, thinking that the head will replace it. If indeed there is such a thing as the science of education, it is above all a science in which the brain of the heart plays a vital role.

But the head can orient you toward the intelligence of the heart just as, in the beginning, the head orients you toward the intelligence of the body. You were taught to walk, to grasp objects, to do physical exercises. And every human being ought to have sufficient education of the heart to be able to "perceive" a child and to be an educator himself. It is the heart alone which will give the right, scientific, rigorous response like a computer. Only the heart can *know* for certain, as long as it functions well.

We always try to avoid that which shows how important it is to work on the emotions. This is because when you are twenty, twenty-five or thirty years old, you look at how long it took to get an education. It took from the first grade when you began to read and write, up to your master's degree. If you are an expert in a physical activity, you realize how much time it took to become one. And now, perhaps at the age of forty, you see that if it took fifteen years of study, plus several years of work on your own outside college (reading books, perfecting a foreign language, studying philosophy and metaphysics)—and if it took so many years to develop physically—then just as much work will have to be done on the emotional brain. That seems an impossible task. So you try to economize on it. And you plunge back into your intellectual study of books by Durkheim, Krishnamurti or Shankara.

You cannot economize on this emotional education. A human being, one worthy of the name, is a "three-brained being." Nature offers you three brains and you only use two. Work on the emotions is not specific to Swâmiji's teaching. From the day I started spiritual research in the Gurdjieff groups, I began specific work on the emotional center. With Mâ Anandamayî, with Ramdas, everywhere—although it was not necessarily obvious—a decreasing of the distorted functionings of the brain of the heart was taking place. This particular work later became more conscious with Swâmiji, but part of it had already been accomplished. Each time you sincerely turn yourself toward spirituality—whether you participate in a ritual or a ceremony, or you meditate in a Buddhist or Christian chapel—you are already undertaking a purification of the emotional brain. Now it must be pushed more intensely, with more precise understanding.

Today I have spoken of these three brains separately, but you must understand that it is their coexistence which makes up a human being. They must each be seen as having separate functions, yet as completing each other. The intelligence of the body grasps one part of the information and processes it, the intelligence of the heart another part of the information, and the intelligence of the head still another part. And it is only in this manner that you can process all the information and supply the action--the complete and right response—in a situation.

Although I took Gurdjieff's astonishing expression "man, a three-brained being" as a starting point, this is in perfect agreement with the Vedantic teachings which insist very strongly on the disappearance of the emotions and on the importance of feeling. And in actual fact, how deformed we all are! It was only with Swâmiji that I became convinced of this. He himself was quite gifted physically—it seems he was athletic in his youth—and he had a presence, a way of situating himself in his body, that was more than convincing. What's more, he was intellectually dazzling. When I saw what an intelligent heart he had, and that his real superiority over all of us was the intelligence of his heart, I was no longer able to doubt. I gave in. I acknowledged that I could not economize on this work on the heart. The simple fact of living beside Ramdas and Mâ Anandamayî had already purified feeling in me. Taking suffering with acceptance, because it is experienced in an ashram, is a beginning. But for me to systematically undertake this education of the "heart" brain, I had needed Swâmiji. The very fact that it hurts just to hear this, shows how badly our hearts function.

Do not delude yourself: it is not because you are full of emotions that your heart functions well. "Oh, but I'm not a dried-up intellectual! I have a heart, I vibrate, participate, love, suffer and get angry." That is the opposite of the intelligence of the heart. Emotions provide you with the raw material on which you can work. Do not smother them, do not repress them, instead transform them, purify them.

The heart as a brain functions properly only as long as there is no emotion. If feeling is the intelligence of the heart, emotion is the stupidity of the heart. We do not have the right to say someone is intelligent if he does not have an intelligent heart—one which is an instrument of understanding, a "brain" capable of perceiving without distorting information, capable of processing the information in its specialty (that of feeling) and capable of knowing with absolute certainty what response to give.

This is why human society is so badly off: families, groups, associations, nations, labor unions, employers' federations, management, government departments, the U.N., UNESCO. That is why, everywhere, there is so much madness and suffering. And at the same time as it is decried by one and all, everyone is an accomplice in his own respective sphere. All over and on all levels, men who hold humanity's destiny in their hands lack intelligence of the heart. At the point of decay this function of knowing has now reached, man is no longer a three-brained being. How can you live, experience, perceive, appreciate situations, decide, act—how can you live, cut off from one of your three brains?

"Brain" should have a very simple meaning for you, that of a specific function which allows you to communicate from outside in to yourself (receiving and perceiving information), and from yourself to the outside (responding to what the situation requires). No response can be given only by the body, only by the head or even by the body and the head together. You cannot dispense with this long and persevering work of purifying the heart. It is up to you to commit yourself or not to commit yourself.

4

MAN AND WOMAN

The issue of our own maleness and femaleness is one that stretches far into our unconscious, involving us so deeply and intimately that we find it difficult to even hear any discussion on the subject.

Both ancient wisdom and modern psychology state that man carries within himself a female component, and woman, a male component. This has been physiologically verified in endocrinology, and it also constitutes one of the most important elements of C.G. Jung's work: the animus and anima. But I wish to speak from the Oriental standpoint.

A Hindu sculpture—*ardhanareshwara*—is half man, half woman. Its right half is male; its left half is female. Since what applies to a Divinity also applies to man, a human being is seen as a representation of total reality. An accomplished man is therefore also *ardhanareshwara*: male and female reunited. A total man has assumed his own female element, and a fulfilled woman has assumed her own male element.

This subject touches on the difference between the sexes, and therefore on relationships between the sexes. Nowadays, the condition of women arouses a multitude of often badly-controlled emotions. Yet certain principles are at work throughout the universe, and they are figuratively expressed in the different mythologies. They operate on the metaphysical, ontological, causal, subtle and physical levels. Indeed, the entire Manifestation is based on the distinction between two forces which are, at the same time, distinct and indissolubly linked.

You have all heard of yin: the female principle, and yang: the male principle. You may also have heard of Purusha, the Unmanifest (male) and Prakriti, Nature (female), or of Shiva (the witness, the unchanging) and Shakti (the dynamic aspect of Shiva). Mythologies, far from being a bunch of infantile fables, are a figurative expression of the great realities that touch simultaneously on our thoughts, feelings and sensations.

The division of humanity into two sexes is therefore the application, on the human level, of the fundamental principles of physical, subtle and causal reality. Actual metaphysical Reality is situated beyond, or rather within, this first differentiation of the essential male and female principles.

It is a fact that when in deep meditation, one no longer feels himself to be man or woman. Central consciousness is so perfectly non-conditioned that it transcends identification with a male or female form. On the level of the ultimate "I," all of this fades away because the atman is neither male nor female. Indeed, the consciousness of certain sages—who spend their days in *samadhi*, apart from an occasional look or word for those surrounding them—is so detached from their appearance, that they no longer feel themselves to be man or woman. But to return to a more accessible level, these two principles that Swâmiji called male and female, are at work in every man and every woman. The female principle prevails in the woman; the male principle prevails in the man.

What is difficult, yet constitutes a large part of the Way to wisdom, is for a man to first of all completely assume his maleness, and a woman her femaleness . . . and then for the man to integrate his femaleness, and the woman her maleness. Granted that much of modern psychology has taken into account the presence of the female element in man, and the male element in woman, it is nonetheless a big step from what is written in books to personal realization. To fully accomplish the plenitude of the human state is no easy task.

So let's go step by step, avoiding latent emotions connected with women's inferiority complex in a so-called phallocratic society, and leaving aside the castration complex, the desire to have a penis or other subjects that may lead to discussion. Unfortunately, today men are rarely men, women are rarely women, and we live in a world dominated by ideas, slogans and prejudices on what makes a man virile or a woman feminine . . . all of which is very far indeed from the completeness to which you are all called.

These female components for a man and male components for a woman do not have to be acquired. They already exist in us— but they need to be liberated and fulfilled, instead of repressed, denied or distorted.

Today, I will leave aside the properly traditional or esoteric aspect of Shiva-Shakti, Purusha-Prakriti, as well as what the spiritual teachings say on ontology, cosmogonies, and the male and female in a universal perspective. Nonetheless, let me start with a well-known Hindu reality . . . one that any traveler to India can observe by looking at the temple statues. It is the famous Shiva lingam: a black stone raised vertically, rarely sculptured to in any way resemble a penis, but generally considered to be a phallus. This lingam is set in a cup-formed base, yoni. Certain observers have rather superficially seen it as an image of the penis penetrating the vagina, assuming it to be a symbol of union or reunion. But the truth is more subtle. The lingam does not penetrate the cup . . . it emerges from it, as the lotus emerges from the mud. It is symbolic of the Manifest (male, dynamic) emerging from the Unmanifest (female, inert).

One who studies the Hindu creation stories, is struck by the contradictions between the different versions. Sometimes water is the primordial element, sometimes fire. Yet despite the differences, it is water or earth (two female elements) which almost always appear as the first principles of differentiation, or of the Manifest. This doctrine of the four elements is precious, and should not be taken for an old pre-logical or primitive superstition. Water and earth are female; air and fire are male. That distinction ties in with the central core of esoteric knowledge.

Hindus consider that the male emanates from the female. This concerns us all, not simply in that the lingam comes forth from a cup called yoni, but because you too can make male elements spring from female elements. Traditional images can be taken with a grain of salt by modern minds, but they do seek to illustrate a principle. Milk is a liquid containing all the properties of water. Nonetheless milk can be churned into butter. And while pouring milk onto fire will extinguish the flames, pouring butter onto fire will feed them. The male butter is therefore present in a latent state in the female milk. You cannot burn water, but water is itself composed of oxygen and hydrogen, both of which are combustible. This will not lead us very far from the point of view of natural science, but symboli-

cally, it is an important image. Another very common representation of the element earth is wood—like the wood of the cross of
Christ. And it is a well-known fact that rubbing two sticks together
creates fire.

Therefore the first thing to understand is that in every human
being, whether man or woman, our male nature emerges from our
female nature. Although this is so both in woman and in man, do
not forget, as simple common sense tells us, that female values
dominate in women, and male values in men. Still, a complete being
should become ardhanareshwara.

***

So many times Swâmi Prajnanpad answered my more or
less intellectual questions with "What does nature say?" Not "What
do the 2500-year-old Upanishads say," but "What does nature say?"
Let's look briefly at what a man is, and what a woman is. It will
help you to understand maleness and femaleness.

What does nature say? Apart from two eyes, a nose, a mouth,
two hands and two feet, man has sexual organs that are visible,
and woman has sexual organs that are non-visible. A woman
possesses the equivalent of a man's sexual organs. Instead of a penis
and two testicles, she has a vagina and two ovaries. But in one case
they are visible, in the other hidden—not visible from the outside.
And what else does nature say? It is not the woman who puts an
ovum into the man's body, but rather the man who puts the sperm
into the woman's body. Nature herself says that man gives and
woman receives.

So far, there is no room for your mind to intervene and deny
such an obvious truth. But we can go further in our effort to
understand ourselves and understand the path to fulfillment and
liberation. Before looking at what makes a man virile and a woman
feminine—something which has become quite difficult in our
neurotic society—we can see that woman receives the sperm emit-
ted by man; therefore woman receives, and takes into herself, while

man gives, and emits out of himself. In the notions female and male, yin and yang, the female aspect is that of reception, welcome, internalization, hidden and profound ripening . . . while the male aspect is one of outer projection.

Both Hindus and Buddhists say that in a series of successive lives, one can be sometimes man, sometimes woman. This could also explain why certain female tendencies are found in a man, and certain male tendencies in a woman. But we can leave aside the viewpoint of successive lives. After all, it is you in this present life who have the chance to be conscious that you are, and so to discover the secret of Being and of Consciousness.

Now let's try to bring these different elements together. The easiest to see is the natural function of procreation; then there is the important Shiva lingam symbol, a non-realistically portrayed phallic emblem, emanating from the cup or yoni. The meaning of this goes beyond--that every human being comes from the mother, is formed in the uterus, and comes into the world at delivery (from the mother's viewpoint), or at birth (from the baby's viewpoint). In the symbolism of the four elements, earth and water correspond to the above. It is effectively within the earth that germination occurs. It also occurs in water, where many life forms multiply, while they do not develop in fire.

There is also the famous image of waves born from the ocean, or that of the Spirit that blows over the Waters in the Old Testament Genesis. It is the wind, a male element, that blows over the water, a female element, and from the water emerge the waves.

Although these ancient comparisons are never perfect, they do have their value as material images used to explain subtle realities. We have to renounce a certain arid, specifically male logic (one that has become distinctive of a caricatured male image) in order to accept this allegorical approach, rich in imagery. I do not need to elaborate on such widely-accepted, archetypal symbolism as the nourishing earth, or the fluidity and adaptability of water. All that is said about the symbolism of water and the earth also applies to female values, whereas all that is said about air (or wind) and fire can teach us much about male values.

The female principle in all human beings is one of depth. All associated with depth is of a female nature. And all that comes from the depths to the surface is of a male nature. Therefore the effort to meditate can be described as essentially female, since it is one of internalizing, going down into one's depths . . . whereas an enterprising mind, action, the desire to shape the world are all essentially male. Nevertheless, action in all well-balanced individuals is born from within. Waves emerge from the ocean, and just action emerges from the deeper zones of one's being.

To come back to what is true both psychologically and physically: man gives and woman receives.

This is fundamental. Impressions and sensations that come from the outside penetrate into us. They touch us, and do so on the female level of our being. This is the same for both men and women. People are generally neurotic in this area, but if we are at all balanced, with each perception, we find ourselves in a female attitude. An outside element penetrates us, then matures and ripens in us—this again is an essentially female process. Next, we respond to the situation, or as it too often happens, we react mechanically; such a response or reaction is essentially male. This sounds so very simple, yet it is the key to both a real comprehension of oneself and to a just relationship between the sexes. If humanity is to be happy, what matters is that women be easily and naturally women, and that men be easily and naturally men.

***

All that welcomes, receives, takes within and lets ripen is female. All that projects, promotes, even procreates (most words starting with pro) is male.

The female aspect precedes the male one because before giving, projecting, expressing . . . one must first receive, carry within oneself.

Perhaps this is new for you. So, what does nature say? For a woman to one day bring a child into the world—an act corresponding in itself to the male aspect of Creation—she must first have received the sperm within the depths of her being, united it to her own substance, and let it mature. This is true on both the physical and psychological levels. Whenever we receive something that can germinate within us, all of us—both we men and you women—have a female attitude. Each time, after carrying something in gestation, we express it outwardly, all of us—both we men and you women—have a male attitude. The male side of existence comes from the female side. A baby comes from the depths of its mother's womb, and each just action comes from the depths of our perception and maturation.

Now, how does this principle work? Here great confusion reigns, because you are all impregnated with superficial ideas about the rivalry of the sexes. "Women's liberation" most often consists in not letting women be real, fulfilled women, but rather in proposing that they be caricatures of men.

To be a complete man is to have assumed one's female component and to be a complete woman is to have assumed one's male component. This is definitely an important point. But the path to perfection for a human being also means a woman should be a complete woman, and a man, a complete man. Our modern world has little by little shaped a society that seems to give supremacy to men—forgetting not only the value of maternity, of which only women are capable, but also progressively forgetting the value of the female principle. Our present society unbalances both us men and you women because it no longer recognizes the primary value of femaleness.

This movement gets worse and worse, nourished on empty ideas that were once true (but have been deformed) or are still true (but are not in their right place). "Woman is intuitive and illogical, man is logical." Do not let yourselves be impressed by such superficial statements. The truth is that the female aspect of a human being does not concern the intellect as we understand it today. Yet to thereby conclude that the female aspect of the human being is inferior—this is the lie from which our modern Western world is dying. As if the male aspect of intellect, mind, and logic had exclusive value . . .

We cannot think, reason, reflect, or deduce unless we have first felt, perceived, and received . . . unless we have been "recep-

tive" like woman in nature, or like the female principle as mani-
fested in creation. However, denying these female values (which
are not logical, Cartesian values) is relatively recent, but disastrous,
for our society. The female aspect of reality—earth, water, the uterus,
receptivity, the depths from which the creative act emerges—has
eminent value.

If now we say that woman is intuitive—perhaps. But that she
is irrational . . . what does that mean? Are we speaking of a complete, affirmed woman or of a diminished, psychologically
wounded, badly-developed, smothered woman, influenced by a
pathologically male society? Yes, the modern world in which we
live is—to use the expression dedicated to it—phallocratic. But that
does not mean that the world gives superiority to men over women.
To understand it so is not to see rightly. It simply means that the
modern world gives superiority to the male cosmic principle over
the female principle. Women pay for this, and so do men. But the
mistake of the feminist reaction is not to challenge this error of
principle. Instead, women do their best to deny the female aspect
of reality in order to equal or beat men in their maleness . . . while
unfortunate men, having lost their femininity, are just as bewildered
as women.

Simone de Beauvoir, echoed by all her successors, wrote in
The Second Sex that this society is less destructive of women and
favorable to men, than it is destructive of the female element in
women and of the female element in men. And a magnified male
element can only lead to neurosis, to being cut-off from oneself,
and hence to alienation. The emotional and sensory level of a human
being, his true sensitivity, is a female characteristic.

Swâmiji said: "Be sensitive." Not in the sense that "the slightest little thing can make you cry," but in the capacity to feel. The
two key words of Swâmiji's teaching were "to feel (feeling)" and
"to see." A sage no longer has emotions, but has become very
sensitive, like a perfected instrument that weighs objects to the
thousandth of a milligram, instead of to the nearest couple of grams.
To see or seeing is the male aspect of a human being, and to feel is
the female one, since one can only feel if one opens up, welcomes,
and takes inside, without protecting oneself.

To use a rather lively image: a woman who closes her thighs in order not to be penetrated can never accomplish the miracle of bringing a new human being into the world. If we close up for fear of outside reality, we deny and smother the female aspect of ourselves. And many human beings today, both men and women, have smothered their sensitivity. Yet they want to act. To do so, they must apply a certain logic to direct their actions. And that logic (a male function) is cut off from perception, which is the foundation of all vision. That logic is invading our modern world.

Proof of this is a grave phenomenon—the proliferation of purely intellectual tests. Cerebral logic has become the unique measure of assessment and selection. Everything goes through the head. Our society is self-destructing because it has suffocated sensitivity and magnified intellectualism. Having suffocated the female values of human reality and magnified male values, we are less and less capable of feeling. Sensitivity is being bruised, repressed, refused and denatured by neuroses. And to make up for this, we have put the accent on intellectual abilities.

What a tragic loss for us all—men and women, all of humanity to see female values renounced, while deviated male values are praised to the heavens. Women no longer dare to be women; they feel that the very thing that makes them so precious to the whole of humanity is without value. They believe that what matters is their capacity to develop their virility, with its corollaries—a logical mind, studies and activism. And women will no longer be called "marvelously illogical."

How can you expect to act, create, produce, change the course of events, and express yourself (male functions) in a just manner, if you are not first open to all that comes to you--not intellectually, but through feelings and the heart? Swâmiji said: "Everything is sexual," but not in the Freudian sense. All duality is sexual: duality means sexuality; non-duality means transcending sexuality. What does sexual mean? It is to receive through an orifice. And the Upanishads speak of the nine orifices: ears, nose, mouth . . . All information penetrates into us through these orifices.

We can see there a female element of opening and reception. To let oneself be penetrated and to receive what penetrates is to manifest the female principle. Yet such receptivity is being progressively diminished. We close up and protect ourselves. We no longer dare to open up to what comes to us through feeling and sentiment—touching us directly in our sensitivity—rather than what comes to us through the intellect. But the input we get through feeling is deposited in us by the outside world, given to us, and it is normal to carry this in gestation. Afterwards, we express, we manifest to the outside world: we become male. When a woman gives birth, even though it is the very image of her function as a mother, she is manifesting her male aspect which "projects outwards" instead of taking within.

A real male is one who has developed the female aspect of his nature, not simply one who has big muscles or who "goes for it," who decides, builds or destroys.

It is fashionable today to speak ironically about the academic elite, but the real source of this irony is that logic is suffocating the capacity to feel. And this leads to disaster. In aid to the Third World, where sensitivity and intuition play a very large role, technocrats do not feel. They think. With their figures, calculations and reason, they displace populations, decide on new crops and destroy a natural balance that men who had not smothered their female values had felt for centuries. A top-level engineer at the French Geographical Institute was here this morning. He told me of startling examples of the Western technocrat's difficulty to understand how an age-old balance has been established, in conditions that are definitely poor, but liveable. This balance was made possible by a sense of feeling and intuition that he himself lacks, because he feels nothing and opens himself to nothing. Yet he arrives with all those ideas he has ingurgitated during his studies in France, and starts to decide what the nomads should do to settle down, and how they must change their methods of breeding, grazing and crop-raising. Unfortunately, the failures and errors accumulate in America, Asia and Africa.

Such incomprehension is the glory of the male sex, and it has become our society's criterion for measuring women. If a woman graduates from a top-level college, what retaliation for the female sex! Is it really women's goal today to prove that they too can become drastically reduced and neurotic men? They could instead become women who have integrated their masculinity, just as we men have to integrate our femininity and to rediscover that sense of reception which is the basis of gestation and creation. It is not necessary to "think logically" when receiving a man's penis and sperm. "What does nature say?" The world would not run so badly if we could create an irrigation system, draw up a city urbanization plan, or establish a new fiscal organization in the same way as a woman creates a baby: by first opening up and letting ourselves be penetrated by reality, which would then work by itself within us.

But if we contemptuously decide that sensitivity is an inferior function reserved to hippies, poets and women, while intelligence is the superior function that produces technicians, scientific researchers and administrators, then we are playing with truth and with Creation itself. "To see," the buddhi (intelligence), and "to feel," are equally precious, and equally necessary.

It is normal that we have associated the uterus—a woman's privileged area, where she can create a new human being—with the idea of depth. In the traditional way of apprehending reality, all the symbolism of depth, with all the wealth that word can include, has naturally been compared to the female organs and therefore to femininity—and that is right. When we speak of depth psychology, we should dare to say the psychology of the female aspect of reality. Depth implies femininity, but modern man and woman are more and more cut off from their depth . . . hence the immense reaction seen in the popularity of modern therapies. It is not easy to rediscover one's own depth. If all those who have done a year of bio-energy or primal therapy were liberated, many of our contemporaries would already be much better off.

Depth psychology therefore means the psychology of the female aspect of the human being—man or woman. Indeed through it, one rediscovers the importance of the capacity to perceive outside influences or impressions. The depth psychology approach does not directly attack the intellect, but instead tries to touch the emotional area, the area of what has been received and felt: "How did I perceive my mother's love, my father's love, my mother's anger, my father's anger? How did I first open myself to the world, and then close up and imprison myself in various protective mechanisms?" Today we are all on the defensive, or we all used to be, because we are afraid to let ourselves be wounded. The emotional is the female level of man, so what kind of man is it who has denied his emotional side, or whose emotional side has become sick?

Swâmiji's own way includes a therapy called lying (memory-recall of unconscious traumatisms), where one no longer resists, but rather descends into one's own depths. This is a female attitude. It saves both men, and women who are no longer women, because it allows them to rediscover the deep irrational, emotional wealth of their being. (In saying irrational, I am not being contemptuous . . . however I would be if I said rational.) "Lying" is one of the possibilities Swâmiji gave us to find our femaleness again, and to dare open up to that very part of ourselves to which we closed ourselves in the past.

A baby opens himself to the world, but after receiving many blows, he closes up and denies all that he has received by thus opening himself . . . all the sufferings and deceptions. They are all repressed. A child is cut off from his depth, from what he feels, and be it a little boy or a little girl, the child gives more and more importance to his intellect by reading, reading, and reading—as if reading a book on swimming could replace the joy of splashing about in a pool. Both the little girl and the little boy must first of all be good students. That is what is measured and appreciated. But if his or her emotional side is non-existent, society takes no account of it. It is the individual himself, pushed by his sufferings, who will later turn to a psychotherapist or possibly to a guru.

If you have denied your femaleness, you become abnormal . . . and some have become so abnormal that they have centered their spiritual quest on their loss of openness and on their refusal of what was engraved in them while they were open. And so everything goes through the head . . . with one more book on the Sufis, and one more book on Zen, one more book on meditation, and one more book on the Vedanta . . . You can also read all of Freud without ever doing any analysis, or juggle with the Oedipus complex, castration, and the anal and oral stages, to better protect yourself against your own unconscious. Depth psychology is the rediscovery of your female potentialities.

The creative struggle of man (who modifies the face of the earth, who organizes, decides, decrees a code of law, sets up a society, governs a firm . . . all the activity that we associate with maleness today) is only right if it is initially the expression of a total opening, "a state of beingness" as Gurdjieff said, to reality. One of the astrological signs dominant in my own chart, and occupied by many planets, is Gemini; it is an intellectual sign that stimulates male values: establishing contacts, traveling, organizing meetings, and doing commerce (in either ideas or fabrics); I had to rediscover little by little the falseness of the values in which modern society had raised me, and in particular, that life did not consist in being a good student. I have often enough emphasized that the lyings were only a small part of Swâmiji's teaching, and yet they saved me insofar as they helped me to completely accept my own depth and irrationality, and to recognize all I had lived through and felt since my childhood.

A man who is exiled from his femaleness is not a real man, even if he portrays more and more of that maleness which has no root in depth, and even if he becomes (in the deplorable sense of the terms) more and more virile, logical and implacable . . . a technician, cut off from his sensitivity and always immersed in books, figures and statistics. When a man has excessively suppressed his femaleness—or a woman, her maleness (her capacity to create, reflect and produce)—then both the man and the woman become particularly vulnerable to the opposite sex because they are desperately looking for that dimension of life which should normally exist in themselves. That is also what makes you so fragile.

Last evening, Marco had the courage to say: "Many women have told me 'I love you' during my life, yet I am convinced I have never been loved"; this is true for most of you men because, in a woman, you are looking for that femaleness which you do not dare to discover in yourselves. The more you cut yourselves off from your own femaleness, the weaker you become to women. You are afraid of this weakness, you are on your guard, you react with hardness and, as it is said so well today, you transform a woman into an object in order to render her harmless.

Furthermore, if you men have repressed or destroyed your own intuitive, irrational femaleness, then you are attracted to women—yet you are also afraid of them, because they represent that which you fear within yourselves. The well-known fear of women, there in the heart of every man, will actually disappear if you accept your own necessity to feel, to become "sensitive," to open yourselves without reservation to the wind, the rain, a birdsong, ascent—to open all your senses to impressions and perceptions. If you have the strength to rediscover your emotions, to become receptive, intuitive, irrational, "childlike" again, you will no longer fear the female part of yourselves, and therefore the female part imminent in women. You will escape both the fascination which makes you childish in front of women, and also the fear.

As for women, it is certain that they will only be fully human if they also develop male values—those corresponding to the symbolism of air and fire. Yet for a woman to be able to embody these male values, she must first have assumed her own female ones. If she also ends up afraid of her sensitivity, of her capacity to communicate and to make love with the entire universe, then her male side will be pathological. If a woman smokes three packs of cigarettes a day and if, harassed by the ringing of three telephones, she is glad to have men under her in the company where she works . . . has she completely fulfilled her existence? All of this sounds basically simple enough, but it is much more difficult to feel. You see, you all protect yourselves against your emotional side—though you do it badly, because the emotional submerges you all the more since you do not give it its place in your lives. Female values make a real man. Yet in maintaining the difference between man and woman, I do not consider the woman inferior, nor have I ever denied that male capacities were accessible to women.

Come back again to the astonishing idea that when a woman gives birth, she acts in a male way . . . because she is procreating, producing a new human being. In fact, men also try to "give birth." Two technicians do not hesitate to say: "How is our baby?" when talking about their project, even if it is the new car Peugeot is putting

out. Or else: "That's it! I spent all night at it, but I finally got it out."
Language is revealing in these cases. When a woman gives birth,
she acts in a male way—she changes something on the face of the
earth. She may not have built the Tower of Montparnasse (the
highest office building in Paris) or the Southern Autoroute, but
she has put together the "precious human body" of a future adult.

To use Swâmiji's expression, a woman also acts in a male way
when, as in the past, she is "queen in her kingdom"—in the house,
or the home in the old sense of the term. Even by staying within
the realm traditionally attributed to a woman, she was able to fulfill
herself by manifesting her male aspect in reflecting, organizing,
directing, and reigning over hearts. In civilizations less diseased
than ours, men perfectly accepted the authority of women in many
spheres. The woman decided, and the man let her direct. And of
course, there have obviously always been exceptional cases of
women qualified for power. India has had numerous sovereigns
carrying out male dharmas, from ancient times up to Indira Gandhi.

If at least women still respected female values . . . but ever
since their childhood, these values have been made suspect. Do you
think it is easy for a little girl to hear it said to a little boy: "Don't
cry—only girls cry"? How ridiculous! Not only do boys end up
repressing their sensitivity and becoming no more than a brain cut
off from their heart and from their feelings, but women themselves
accept that "girls cry, of course, because they are only girls," while
little males do not cry. There is no doubt that, if women let themselves be influenced by such prefabricated ideas, they no longer
dare to be women. And if they were not very good students, if they
did not graduate from high school with honors, they feel inferior.
Indeed, a civilization that puts studies and the intellect above all
else is a morbid and schizophrenic civilization.

Do you want to become well again? Do you want to be healthy
cells in this dying society? Then do not make a pact with this modern
world's illness . . . dare, as men, to rediscover your femaleness and,
as women, to honor it. A well-balanced humanity absolutely needs
the union of its men and women, not their competition.

A real couple is one in which the man is grateful to the woman
for helping him to assume the female part of himself, and the woman

is grateful to the man for helping her develop her male side. As long as men deny their female side—and women do likewise because of the prevailing ideas of our society—life in the couple will continue to be just as jeopardized as it is today . . . filled with a never-satisfied hope, crushed love, misunderstandings, quarrels and intense sufferings. It is tragic when we realize what plenitude and beauty a relationship between a man and a woman could hold. Life in the couple is only possible for a man who completely accepts his femaleness, and for a woman who not only completely accepts her maleness, but who also completely accepts her femaleness . . . because even women no longer dare to accept it today.

What is really serious today is that female values are renounced, decried, and scorned . . . at least in fact, if not in word. We are dying from this loss, while all the alleged remedies (starting with women's liberation) lie within the aberration itself. The only glimmer of hope comes from modern psychology's rediscovery of the importance of the emotional world. Unfortunately, we only rediscover this emotional world once it no longer functions. We discover it as we would an illness; indeed, the word "affect" in modern psychology designates an emotional malfunction.

The emotional world is of prime value. Everything else comes after it. First feel fully, and then see what should be done . . . no longer "reacting," but instead "responding." Happy the man who can fully acknowledge that all his diplomas are not worth a woman's capacity to feel, to open herself, and to take inside the messages the world gives us; happy he who understands that a woman has a different way from his of adapting herself to the world . . . a way that is just as valuable.

As long as men continue to look down on their own sensitivity, to be open to the outer world only to dominate it, instead of letting it permeate them and communing with it, curing our society will be impossible. At most, a few individuals may escape the general decadence.

Nehru cannot be considered a traditional Indian. But he had nevertheless the typically Indian reaction of protesting the triumphal declaration: Everest has been "defeated" or "conquered." This statement is an example of essentially male behavior . . . the male attitude, deprived of female roots, only considers nature as an opponent to conquer. Instead, Nehru said: "Everest has become our friend," as if we had made its acquaintance. But men and women cut themselves off today from being receptive to the messages of nature. This is a material loss to which ecologists are trying to attract our attention. Yet even worse, it is a human and spiritual loss.

To commune with Nature, the great universal Life, is the fundamental attitude. It is only from here that right action can come—the action of a sage who has fully developed in himself the complete female dimension of humanity. The sage can understand. To understand is to include. Be you man or woman, dare to give back pre-eminence to all the female values, wherever these values come from . . . myths, allegories, parables, or symbols. Impregnate yourselves with these female values. Then, at last, the real path of happiness will open before you.

5

MALE AND FEMALE

Let us here go further into this theme of male and female. The first point to realize is that this subject is metaphysical and theological as well as psychological and physical. The laws and principles which underlie the manifest universe govern all levels of the Manifest; in reality, the division of humanity into two sexes is simply an application of this great principle, which we will call the male and the female.

The modern approach starts from the ordinary level to explain the higher levels; it well-nigh considers that all spiritual doctrines are idealistic projections or symbolizations of biological facts. Starting from the observation that men have a penis and women a vagina, if you follow a certain line of thought (such as the relationship between father and daughter, or mother and son), you can proceed to elaborate a whole system explaining religious ideas. This is what many psychoanalysts have done.

On the other hand, one can acknowledge the truth of the traditional teachings. The Manifest is a progressive process of densification, starting from the Origin. In the Unmanifest, it is first the causal plane which appears, then the subtle plane and finally the physical plane. These three levels are also found in each one of us. The principles which govern the transition from the Unmanifest to the Manifest are at work at all stages of reality, and on all the interior planes of a human being. This explanation, found in the different esotericisms—Sufi, Hindu, Christian, Tibetan and Judaic—radically changes our approach to the commonplace daily reality of our lives, which are the concrete expression of spiritual realities.

This is why sexuality has almost always been regarded as sacred; indeed it is why sexuality—or, in any case, sexual symbolism—has played such an important role in many spiritual teachings. No one is now ignorant of the fact that, among various other sculptures, the façades of certain Indian temples depict all possible sexual positions, even including homosexual ones. And the text of the Kama Sutra, famous to the present day as an erotic work, is in fact a voluminous treatise composed by a sage, with one part—and one part only—which deals with the technique of sexual union between man and woman.

Every detail of what we do (even of the activity which we have in common with animals, our sex life) is the expression of a spiritual reality. All we do can therefore be seen as sacred—an epiphany revealing to us the "principles" to which sages or yogis have access during their meditations and states of higher consciousness. By the same token, the division of humanity into men and women (which nowadays gives rise to so much discussion, so many books, televised debates and interviews) can likewise be considered as the expression of a spiritual, causal and subtle reality, before it becomes a physical one. Only by situating the question in this overall context, by seeing it in its completeness, can you rightly understand it. Duality or bipolarity—male and female—is found in nearly every page of the ancient texts or every theme taken up by traditional teachings.

To affirm the ego is to deform the male attitude; to efface the ego is a female attitude. Spiritual life, a sadhana (even though the word sadhana means making efforts), is a receptive attitude—an attitude of openness and not one of affirmation. But how difficult it is for men to accept the idea that they must become much more available to female values than they are! This is a rediscovery, indeed it is the greatest we all can make: it is our capacity to fully recognize the value of this female attitude that will save us. But I must be careful when I speak, each sentence pronounced awakens echos in you of thoughts which are only quotations, of emotions which are only imitations, and of alienating cultural influences.

In all that is peddled about man as a male and woman as a female, there is a mixture of prejudice and truth. And even though this is widely recognized, they nonetheless make their effect. An English proverb, often cited by Indians, says: "Don't throw away the baby with the bathwater." Be careful, when you want to rid yourself of habits or ideas which you consider corrupt, not at the same time to throw away truths which may prove precious if we give them back their eternal freshness by dusting off the banality into which they have fallen. The female attitude corresponds to receiving; the male attitude corresponds to giving. Take this truth as a basis for some thorough reflection to lead you beyond clichés and commonplace ideas to an understanding which, instead of remaining intellectual, will transform your being, your life, and lead you to "Realization." It is a double movement, like breathing: getting and giving. When you inhale, you get; when you exhale, you give. Plants too inhale and exhale, get and give. One cannot exist without the other. Each time a process goes from the outside to the inside, you get; each time the dynamism goes from the inside to the outside, you give. For example, we say "to give blows with a pickaxe." We do not offer a gift to the earth by giving it blows with a pickaxe, and yet we use the expression "to give," implying that we are asserting or expressing ourselves. Every existence—human existence among others—is founded on this double movement: receiving and replacing. Man is a receiving instrument for different coarse and subtle foods, for different energies. He is a transforming instrument and a transmitting instrument, although this instrument is not the same in an ordinary man as it is in a sage. We also transmit vibrations and exteriorize energy.

You have heard it said that woman tends to be passive and man tends to be active. Yes . . . but exactly what is implied by those two words, passive and active, words essential to the translation of Hindu and Buddhist conceptions? Passive seems to mean lazy, it is therefore pejorative; active, on the other hand, is a virtue. If I use the common statement, "man represents the active pole and woman the passive pole," it seems to be an insult for women. In truth, what is active is in no way superior to what is passive. Food for thought can also be found in the surprising words of Ramana Maharshi: "A sage's passiveness is a thousand times more active than ordinary activity." Passiveness merits our respect because passiveness is creative.

Let us return to Swâmiji's starting point, without any prejudices about women's oppression or liberation, "What does nature say?" The most important accomplishment of the human race is to bring another man or another woman into the world, with the idea (long-forgotten for us, but still found among traditional peoples) that this man or this woman will perhaps be a sage—one of the beacons of humanity. In a traditional civilization, every pregnant woman tries to pray, to purify herself in order to be worthy of being the receptacle for a future sage. But since no one is very interested in saints any more (apart from calendar feastdays), I wonder how many men and women copulate with the sacred feeling that they are perhaps going to give a physical body to such a precious human being . . . one as precious as fire for prehistoric man.

And this procreation takes place in a passive manner. A woman can perhaps increase her diet of proteins or mineral salts, but she does not have to set to work in order to create a child. You can roll up your sleeves to dig a trench, or to build a wall in a day, but that is not how a woman procreates.

In this passive attitude, a woman contents herself with receiving: she receives oxygen from the air, she receives different material foods (proteins, glucides, lipids and others) and she receives emotional foods. *Sarvam annam*: "everything is food." That with which a pregnant woman nourishes herself is very important. Does she nourish herself on detective stories or on religious books, on sacred music or on everyday television programs? Among other things, does the woman nourish herself and her child on tar and nicotine by smoking all the more, regardless of the embryo she is carrying within her womb?

Swâmiji told some of us an unlikely story, which he seemed to take quite seriously. A young man of twenty, belonging to a respectable family, committed a crime—and his mother remembered that, during her pregnancy, she had read a book which exactly described the very crime committed by her son twenty years later. Now Swâmiji, who had nonetheless been a physicist and not an occultist eccentric, maintained that there was a link between the fact that the woman had been so marked by the book (even in India such a mistake can occur), and the fact that twenty years later her son committed the crime which had been engraved in him, as a *samskara*, while he was a fetus.

I must admit that in spite of my respect for Swâmiji and his prestigious career as a physicist at the University of Calcutta, I found it difficult to accept that assertion. My intention, in mentioning this today, is not to dwell upon the story itself but instead to remind you how much the procreative attitude of a woman expecting a baby is a receptive attitude. She receives the three foods: food one eats, food from the air (*prana*, as Indians say) and impressions. And in India, great pains are taken so that only subtle, refined impressions will make their mark upon the mother during pregnancy.

As this receptive attitude comes to a close, the woman gives birth. And here her attitude becomes male. The very moment a woman brings a child into the world (especially if she does so consciously—adhering consciously to the contractions instead of letting herself be carried away by the pain), she is performing a male action. She is creating, procreating, acting in the world. This is also true when she breastfeeds the child, even though the most feminine image possible is that of a mother looking tenderly at the baby held to her breast.

***

Now we can go a little further. You agree that all well-balanced human beings, be they men or women, normally have these two attitudes of giving and receiving, letting themselves be transformed and transforming. Yet today, both as men and as women, you are much more oriented toward the attitude and the behavior which consists in transforming, rather than in letting yourselves be transformed. You are afraid to be passive and have given priority to activity. Yet passivity is just as important as activity. Any harmonious human being is capable of passivity. You must rediscover how to receive without protecting yourself; you must dare to make yourself vulnerable and let yourself be transformed.

This is a directive found in many ancient teachings: to let oneself be transformed by the action of the Holy Spirit within, to let oneself be transformed by the action of Grace within. In spiritual life, it is necessary at the same time to make much effort (this is called a sadhana in Sanskrit) and to have this passive attitude on which all mystics have insisted . . . to open oneself to the influence of the Holy Spirit, to open oneself to the influence of Grace, to open oneself to the revelation of the Atman.

The limited cannot seize the Unlimited, the finite cannot seize the Infinite, the ego cannot seize the supra-individual, the mind cannot seize the supra-rational, the minus cannot seize the plus. You can only let go and open yourself. And that has become practically impossible for you. You modern men and women are on the defensive; you can only count on your own strength. *Surrender* is a word very much used in India. You have to be completely saturated with the Teachings of Ramana Maharshi or other sages to start hearing with a more favorable ear that the paramount, the optimum, is *surrender*, capitulation. Capitulation to whom and to what? Either you capitulate to your unconscious and to your mind—which completely direct you today—or you capitulate to God himself who, in the metaphysical perspective, is your fundamental Reality, your supreme Self, even though you are unaware of it.

At the time when I was confusedly starting to catch a glimpse of these truths, because I was effectively starting to open myself to the Hindu teachings (before I met Swâmiji), I wrote in the little book named *Yoga and Spirituality:* "We do indeed want everything—but it must be *us.*" "I" am there to act: to hold my arms outstretched for ten minutes even if it hurts, to get up at three in the morning to attend matins services, to inhale through one nostril and exhale through the other, or to prostrate myself three hundred times in a row. We do indeed want to make all the efforts of the sadhana—at least in moments of enthusiasm and fervor—but it must be *us.* *Letting go,* abandoning the ego has to be totally rediscovered.

Back again to the fundamental starting point: "What does nature say?" In this essential act of procreating a human being, a woman makes herself receptive. First of all, receptive to a man. Aside from test-tube babies or other future discoveries of modern science, fertilization comes about through penetration. A woman opens herself to being penetrated by a man. If she is totally and perfectly open, orgasm can even have spiritual value. It is said in an Upanishad that "the Sage lives in permanent orgasm." Do these words have meaning? What meaning can they have? A woman opens herself to being penetrated by a man; the uterus opens itself to receive the sperm. It is an attitude of non-protection.

All Yoga is inevitably a way of opening, of letting things happen, of letting the forces which surpass the ego act in ourselves. There you find a point which you will all have to meet along the course of your Way, assuming you are truly committed to a Way and not simple amateurs. It is the moment when you must renounce the fact that it is you yourself—even at the price of great efforts— who will conquer your Liberation, a moment when you cannot have any other attitude than the female one . . . doing nothing more than opening yourself, making yourself available.

Balancing between the female and the male, receiving and giving, passive and active human life is also a harmony of yes and no. You can see that yes is a female attitude, and no is a male attitude. Each time a woman says no, she manifests the male aspect of her nature; each time a man says yes, he manifests the female aspect of his nature.

Perhaps you recall a little story I have told, which was a revelation for me on the subject of "Yes." I was about to settle down in the center of France, and went to the television studio for the last time, to record the presentation of the Sufi films programmed for screening in September 1974. Arriving on the set a little early, I saw a group of technicians assembled in a corner of the studio, listening to something. But what? Some had already worked with me, others knew me by name and, seeing how interested they were, I approached and asked: "What are you listening to?"

"Ah," one of them answered, "this is not for you; it's a complete change from your India and your sages!" It was an extraordinary purple passage, as they say in the trade, of an actress expressing the unfolding of the sexual act, with startling eroticism, using only the word "yes." On the level of the artist's performance, it was admirable; without her talent, it would have been as vulgar as a pornographic magazine. But this was not the case. From the first series of yesses which were gay, playful, coaxing, then more troubled, up to the final series of grave, husky, moaning, elated yesses, you could follow the entire unfolding of a love encounter.

All using nothing more than the word yes. And while the others listened to that as a "porno" recording, I myself, while recognizing the unparalleled talent of the actress, heard only the word yes: yes, yes, yes. I was saturated with Hindu and Tibetan teachings on erotic symbolism as spiritual symbolism, and saturated also by that word yes, Swâmiji's yes. The ultimate Yes appearing through the yes of a woman giving herself.

Are there still many women capable of totally giving themselves, therefore free of unconscious fears? If those fears remain, the gift cannot be a veritable and total one, without ulterior motives. And who can declare that he is free of the unconscious fear of giving himself? Human sexuality is almost always unsatisfactory, through lack of the right attitude. The mind attempts a compromise which cannot succeed--giving oneself without giving oneself. To say yes is to open up, it is to no longer protect oneself.

Of course, a human being—man or woman—must also say no. The balance of a human existence is in the male and the female, the passive and the active, the yes and the no. This does not put into question the "yes to what is" . . . Aum . . . Amen—the foundation not only of the entire edifice of Swâmiji's Teaching, but of all spirituality. There even exists a Notre Dame of the Yes. Christian life is based on the most famous yes of all—the Virgin's consent at the Annunciation: "I am the Handmaid of the Lord; be it done unto me according to your word." Mary incarnates the female dimension of humanity. She is the disciple's model; all Christian mystics choose Mary as their inspiration, whether they are men or women. It is in no way dishonorable for a man to take a female attitude as a criterion, in order to fully become a man instead of a caricature who only accepts half of reality. Could a human being who consents to exhale but does not want to inhale, survive?

To what will we say yes; to what will we say no? Yes to what is. It is this "yes to what is" which dissolves the breach with total life; it dissolves the prison of the ego which the emotions represent. And each time we put the teaching into practice—when we say "YES, IT IS" because it is, here and now—we have a female, receptive, open attitude. And then we act, but on the basis of this adherence to reality, on the basis of that non-duality expressed in

Hinduism or Buddhism by statues of divinities sexually mating.

Afterwards you can have a male attitude, be you man or woman, and try to transform that which can be transformed, but on the basis of communion and participation and not refusal, contradiction and revolt (that is, emotion). I can transform. IT IS, and I will try to change it. I am ill, YES, and I will try to get better. Trying to get better is a way of saying no to the fact of being ill, but this male no comes after the female yes. Human life is made up of this balance of yes and no. And indeed you can feel that the yes comes first; the no is right only if it comes after the yes. YES, I am sick, feverish, aching, nauseous. NO, I will not sink into this sickness—I will try to get better. It is simple, too simple for the complexity of the mind.

The female attitude precedes the male attitude; the male attitude, without the female attitude, is false. "I do not accept being sick" deprives us of the essential, of the beauty of the yes. Whether it be in response to sickness or to any other unfortunate situation which is nonetheless reality, here and now—that yes, in itself, has a value that most of you do not yet suspect. Saying yes is a way of saying "Enter." When someone knocks at the door, some answer "enter" and others say "yes," meaning "yes, you can enter." It is effectively a female attitude . . . enter.

"Enter." Open up always . . . it is always God who is knocking. That is the discovery of mystics, one unknown to those who continue to live simply in the light of their own minds, a veiled light passing through deforming glass.

Until now (I have been able to verify it day after day), this "yes to what is" still seems too much like resignation to you, like accepting defeat. "I have to capitulate, reality has got the better of me." If in your hands you hold an official paper telling you to pay a much higher sum of taxes than what your tax inspector led you to expect or a traffic ticket much worse than you imagined, say "yes"—with true understanding—say yes: "because it is, and there is no use denying it." But you do not yet know that the fact of saying yes is, in itself, miraculous. That word yes is the springboard which projects you into the state of consciousness for which you are searching through meditation, prayer, breathing exercises and concentration techniques. It is the fullness of "yes" which can give orgasm to a woman or to a man, and it is the fullness of "yes" which can make life a permanent orgasm, to use the expression of the Upanishad.

But what yes will we say? It is the yes itself which should take on new meaning; it should be as total as that of the freest and the most deeply in love woman, giving herself to the man she loves. Open up always—it is always God who is knocking. Everything works toward the good of those who love God. The mind sees either good or bad, but the vision of Truth sees only good. From the moment *it is,* I say *yes.* Everything rests on the fullness of your yes. This yes should no longer be considered a resignation, a defeat. Say yes wholeheartedly to what is apparently only the defeat of the ego, to what is, in truth, always a victory for our inner wisdom and our inner freedom.

This yes you are to furnish should become a religious act. From the standpoint of ordinary intelligence, it is clear that adhering to reality will make emotions disappear and that it is certainly an enormous freedom to be free of emotions. Still, this yes does not fall under the category of psychology, but of trans-psychology, of metapsychology. It depends on the manner in which you understand it, the manner in which you live it, on the way your whole being says yes to what is. Yes is always a cry of victory or the sign of victory, even if it is saying yes to the certainty of having cancer or to the death of one we love.

It is here, and nowhere else, that the secret of what is called spiritual life is to be found. But this is more difficult for modern man to accept than it was for men of the past. In days gone by, this yes (be it that of Islam, Hinduism or Christianity) found its natural expression because the female values of humanity were less held up to ridicule than they are today, and the overdevelopment of male attitudes—and of saying no—had not yet reached its present state.

Since prehistoric times, man has not stopped saying no—no, I will not be cold this winter: I will wear animal skins, sleep in caves instead of outside, keep up the fire lit by lightning instead of letting it go out. Man has never stopped saying no—no to injustice—no to oppression. Such is the male attitude of humanity, but in what manner, with what attitude, and with what overall understanding?

***

"No" has its role to play in human life, but it must be evenly balanced with "yes," just as the male must balance with the female, as opening must balance with projection, receiving with action, letting oneself be transformed with transforming one's outer environment. It is not a case of eliminating the word no from your vocabulary, but rather of eliminating it from your feelings, thereby little by little escaping emotions, so as to one day escape them definitively.

It is normal for the body to say no: if you accidentally put your hand on a burning hot-plate, the body says no and you take your hand away. It is normal for the head to say no: if you order two-inch metal girders and you are delivered girders of a smaller diameter, you say no, you refuse. The head says yes, the head says no; the body says yes, the body says no. But the heart is destined to always say yes. However each time there is a negative emotion (that is, an emotion denying something), the heart says no. And certain emotions seemingly based on a yes are not based on a calm and peaceful yes, but on an excessive yes. You get carried away by a happy emotion but this is just as pernicious in your life as an unhappy emotion.

The right attitude is to respond with an unemotional yes, one from which the mind takes away nothing and to which it adds nothing . . . a YES which is synonymous with the word IS. In religious language, one would say YES; in non-dualistic metaphysical language, one would say IS (the Sanskrit *asti* of the Upanishads). The purified heart always says "yes—it is." The body says no, the head says no, but when the word no disappears on the level of the heart, emotion itself disappears and there is an awakening of what is called feeling (although we would have to be quite clear about the meaning we give to that word). This is the essence of all spiritual life—whether you call it submitting to Divine Providence, adhering to Reality or "destruction of the mind" (*manonasha*).

Look at how this essential theme of non-duality in daily life is directly linked to that of male and female. The maleness of the woman and the femaleness of the man are only the reflection of the male principle and the female principle on all levels of the Manifest. And here lies your difficulty compared with those who have preceded you in past centuries: no longer being on the defensive and consenting to be passive. This is an attitude which is little by little disappearing from our being; if you take the trouble to verify what I am saying, you will see that this is even more true than you imagine. For me, it was a rediscovery which spread out over twenty-five years. I must admit that my familiarity with India or with other Asian civilizations helped me very much.

I can also pay homage to the Gurdjieff teachings—the first I allowed to act in my existence—teachings I will never renounce. Without understanding at the start all that it included, I was proposed a type of effort which was not the usual one. It was an effort of non-effort, in the form of exercises of progressively deeper muscular relaxation, conscious breathing and opening myself to vibrations we are not normally aware of but which we can become conscious of through exercise. For fifteen years, I practiced exercises of silence, relaxation and receptivity with unfortunately only partial results, because the *vasanas* and *samskaras* were too strong in my unconscious to allow me to work them out uniquely by those methods. A long, slow transformation with numerous retreats and many ups and downs was necessary, so that I could better integrate the female values or the female aspect of my being, and no longer be marked by images of an active hero, but instead understand how much and in what manner the sage is greater than the hero.

The models engraved in our subconscious from childhood and adolescence are models of "no." A religious education on the other hand offers us Mary's supreme example of openness in her consent to the Angel. But how many of you can say you are true Christians? As Gurdjieff taught, a Christian is not one who says or believes himself to be a Christian, he is one who has a Christian being. To have a Christian being is to have the being of Mary—the disciple's model—and to say yes to what transforms us.

Oh, it seems easy to us to say yes to the fact of bringing Jesus Christ into the world, but if we really look into what is meant in the traditional teachings of the Church, the young girl Mary—who was a virgin and did not know her fiancé—first of all had to accept being pregnant. That is a point of view which we generally do not consider. And, if you remember something of the Gospels, Joseph was scandalized in the beginning. Whether or not you believe in Mary's virginity is secondary. I am speaking here about the teaching itself, the myth (in the most noble sense of the term), the teaching which can lead you to Liberation. From all of which you ceaselessly protect yourself, from all of which you close yourself off—all that seems to be unhappiness, disappointment, failure and suffering—could transform you in the way you desire. I am proposing an inner conversion, a revolution, the reversal of everything the ego and the mind take as certain. "That which is wisdom in the eyes of man is folly in the eyes of God, and that which is folly in the eyes of man is wisdom in the eyes of God." Yes to whatever comes, to transform us in the real sense of the word: to lead us beyond form.

What is knocking at the door? Sickness? YES. First the receptive attitude—perfect, total. Then the male aspect of reality intervenes and you enter into a struggle against the sickness. The same Swâmiji who used to say *"accept, accept"* in English, also used to say *"it cannot be tolerated."* Accept—in a perfect, mystical, metaphysical way—the thing to which in a moment, in another manner, you are going to say no. This point is not yet completely clear for some of you.

Let us keep the example of being sick. Some have maintained the absolute religious attitude through to the end, entrusting even their recovery to God: "If it is God's will that I become sicker and sicker, and that I die—amen; if it is God's will that I get better, He will cure me." But Mâ Anandamayî herself said: "It is God's will that you be ill, but it is also God's will that there is a doctor near the ashram." Assuming that you are determined to look after yourself (therefore to say no to illness), can you first say a total yes—without reserve and without restriction—to the illness itself, to the visible symptoms, to the X-ray on which the great white marks veil a lung?

This yes must be perfect. It is always a yes of victory, never a yes of defeat. You can express it in religious terms: "I see the will of God in everything; God comes to me through suffering; all God does is for my good; I do not even know what is good or bad for me; will some good not come from this accident, this illness or this professional failure?" On the Way, everything works toward the good of those who love God. You must rediscover that this submission is not your weakness but rather your strength, and that the so-called men in today's world are becoming weaker and weaker. A mere nothing demolishes them, a grimace, a wounding remark, a mishap, a professional failure. A mere nothing demolishes them-and all in the name of strength.

Everything is linked to this theme. It is the very essence of the Way. It can be found in Christianity as well as in the teachings revealed by Count Karlfried von Durckheim on the *hara:* give up trying to pull in your stomach and throw out your chest; accept to go down into your center of gravity in the abdomen. It is not easy. By favoring one aspect of reality, modern man has moved farther and farther away from the true nature of the *hara.* Various works by Karlfried von Durckheim depict photographs of medieval statues with what art historians call the "Gothic belly," proving that this right attitude was known and lived in the Middle Ages. And yet, even if intellectually you are convinced that it is necessary to let go with the head and that the lower abdomen is important, the *hara* at first seems suspicious to you. Because we all have a visceral, fundamental, unconscious fear of what cannot be seen.

Rediscovering one's abdomen and renouncing the head's dictation is the beginning of salvation. As for the heart, it is so cluttered with emotions that you can hardly count upon it. For a long time, the heart imposes its law on you, in the form of attraction and repulsion—driving you crazy with joy or crazy with sorrow. In both cases, the heart drives you crazy. And this is the opposite of Wisdom.

The *hara* exercise is a magnificent balance of the female attitude and the male attitude. The female attitude is there in the release—you let your sense of gravity drop down into the abdomen and no longer try to stick out your chest to affirm your ego. A woman's genital organs are located in her abdomen; it is also in her abdomen where the great work of pregnancy takes place. And at the same time, the *hara* practice is also a practice of the masculine type because it demands active concentration of the attention and a certain pressure on the abdominal muscles. That is why this exercise is so important not only in Japanese Buddhism but also in Tibetan Buddhism (at least for the *kargyu-pa*). To unite the male and female within ourselves, to unite the active and passive within ourselves, is to unite in ourselves the two poles of the Manifest-it is to truly become a Man. As soon as we deny that "what is, is," we pull in the stomach, we are incomplete and we are therefore weak.

The limitation of individual consciousness (*ahamkara* in Sanskrit, translated as ego) is founded on the word no. A child grows up and affirms himself saying no: this is the ordinary human condition. But if you want to escape the ordinary human condition and attain what has been called awakening, wisdom, illumination, the Kingdom of Heaven . . . then you must become female. You must open yourself, you must consent to receive, let yourself be transformed, drop the ego and drop logic. And to do this, you will have to drop fear. A human being lives in fear, and from this ensue all imaginable compensations, on all levels, to anesthetize this fear. The more fear decreases, the more we are able to open ourselves. And the more we open up and see that instead of being destroyed, we are discovering inner security—the more fear diminishes.

What will be your starting point? Your starting point can be intellectual in the beginning. Perhaps the rigor and logic of the Vedantic Teachings appeals to you; this conviction leads you deep into yourself, inciting you to give your heart predominance. The mind is superficial; the heart is deep.

Or if you have a religious temperament, the heart will be touched first. The Christian myth—that of Mary's yes and of Christ himself's yes, the condemnation, crucifixion and resurrection— brings powerful dynamics to life within you, ones on which you can find support and allow to work inside you.

Some have even begun at a physical starting point—it is the language of the body which touched them, the release of the abdomen while exhaling. But in fact you cannot be human unless body, heart and head are convinced, unless they participate together in this work of transformation. You can only be human if you accept the female as much as the male, receiving as well as acting, letting yourself be penetrated as well as penetrating. You can only be human if you consent to rediscover the female dimension. And not only have men lost it, and deplorably so, but women are also in the process of losing it, by letting themselves be influenced by a world which, undeniably, is male in a sinister way.

First of all: YES, then action. What will transform you, what will lead you beyond identification with the *koshas* (the coverings of the Self), what will lead you to the goal, to peace, to non-duality is this YES. Not a yes of defeat, but a yes rich in all your spiritual conviction, in all your metaphysical conviction, in all your mystical conviction, an immense, divine YES . . . even yes to that which is the most mediocre, the most discouraging, the most disappointing. Always YES, because it is always yes to God himself.

6

NON-ACTION

The word *sadhana* implies "making efforts." But obviously the most important question is: what kind of efforts does this mean? How can the ego make efforts which will lead to surpassing the ego? How can the mind make efforts which will lead to the destruction of the mind? Is this not enclosing oneself within a mode of consciousness, only to end up more deeply imprisoned? Ramana Maharshi compared this to a thief who, while escaping, cries "Stop, thief!" in order to divert suspicion, and subsequently turns into a policeman to catch himself!

This is a question which you will sooner or later have to ask yourself especially if you have already put in much sincere effort: "How will the efforts which I make from a certain level of consciousness, lead me beyond that level to liberation, detachment, awakening?" Intense scholastic effort can bring you success in college, and intense physical effort can make you into a great gymnast. But can the kind of effort to which you are accustomed lead you to a different state in which your habitual motivations (your fears and your desires) will drop away? After all, each time we make an effort, we do so with the precise desire of attaining a given goal and a certain result. It is indeed quite a delicate question.

I have already explained that the modern world underestimates female values to an extent which is becoming more and more tragic. You believe that ordinary effort (I want this and therefore I will get it) is what distinguishes one who rises above the crowd. Yet the most important act we can accomplish as human beings—carrying a child within ourselves—is an act which does not correspond to any habitual effort. From this natural fact, various truths can be deduced and verified.

Life only manifests through the alternating of day and night, inhaling and exhaling, action and rest, activity and passivity. There is as much value in passivity as there is in activity—not in passivity made up of torpor, laziness and daydreams but rather in conscious, vigilant passivity. Such an attitude has become more and more foreign to you and this is directly connected to the decline of religious spirit. You are aware that churches are rarely frequented and that there are considerably less vocations to the priesthood, but you do not fully measure the difference which exists between a society like the one in which you have grown up and an ancient society, imbued with religion.

For a certain number of years, I lived in the heart of communities which had remained religious. I am speaking not only of ashrams, monasteries and Sufi brotherhoods, but also of the extremely pure Moslem society which existed in Afghanistan until the present regime, of the Himalayan populations of Tibet, and of Hindus living outside big cities or even sometimes in Bombay or Delhi. All have kept the sense of what is sacred as well as the conviction that man is but one aspect of reality, the other being God, the divine *Shakti* or divine Providence. Except for rare exceptions, modern man (even if he calls himself a Christian) no longer lives his life for God, through God, in God, in the sight of God. These words no longer correspond to *a certainty* or *an experience* which permeates us. But, on the Way of wisdom, even if one follows a Way expressed in non-dualistic, metaphysical language (one where the person-to-person relationship between a creature and a Creator plays no role), the religious mentality itself must inevitably play a determining part. And this mentality which connects us ("connecting" is one of the meanings of the word) implies that we be convinced of the limits to our usual effort and possibilities; it implies our being convinced that we can open ourselves to a force, an influence, which surpasses anything the ego can understand: the smallest cannot contain the most vast, the limited cannot contain the limitless, the finite cannot contain the infinite. If we only take ourselves into account—with our strengths, weaknessess and efforts in their usual form—then we will never succeed.

Everyone—man or woman—who is committed to a spiritual path, is led to harmoniously develop within himself the female aspect of his nature. In relation to the great Reality, Truth or Divine Life, man's attitude is female.

The true mystic, in religious terms, is he who dares to say "I am a woman in love with God"—even if he is a man. Although that may surprise a certain number of you, it is in no way revolutionary for the acknowledged religious traditions. Indeed, the language used by Christian mystics and that found in Hindu devotion is very similar.

Yet today, in a world which is not dominated by men but rather by male values, this female attitude of letting a Force larger than us act is practically forgotten. What does nature say? When a woman conceives and creates a child, she is passive, as passive as is possible. She must not lead an agitated life; at work within her is an energy, a vitality. (I am purposely using vague terms like "energy" and "vitality" in order that each one may find the term which suits him most.) The woman is the place where this work is accomplished. She is not to hinder it, but rather to collaborate. When I say "not to hinder it," this not only means through voluntary interruption of pregnancy, but also through various ways of living which are incompatible with pregnancy. Apart from producing a child, we modern men and women do not understand how we can obtain much outcome by being passive; indeed the idea of "non-action" or "non-acting" (though it is widely known to be central to Taoism) is hardly more than a word for us. What can be the meaning of the statement: "There is nothing which cannot be accomplished through non-acting"? In any case, by means of a woman's non-acting it is certain that an act as admirable as the creation of a new human being can be accomplished.

This is also true on the Path, although there can be many mistakes and misunderstandings in this area. It is not typically religious language which is used here. Never have I criticized Christianity, nor dreamed of turning anyone away from reflecting on the Gospels and Christ's teaching; and though I have often spoken of my numerous stays in a Cistercian Abbey in the west of France, it is the intellectual framework which I found with Swâmiji—the Hindu Vedanta—which is preserved here. Swâmi Prajnanpad was nevertheless a monk, duly ordained by his own guru. He associated himself with the sacred scriptures of India, such as the Upanishads and the Yoga Vashishta; he cited the Mahâbhârata or the Puranas. I have always considered him to be a representative of spirituality and not of modern science or psychology, even though he was an expert in those two domains.

Therefore, if you accept the term "spirituality" (which is the most general and the least provocative of all), you must not forget that what is offered to you here is a face of spirituality which cannot go against the fundamental laws of all spirituality. There is actually a common background even if the ways themselves vary. The common essence is in that attitude we find so difficult to understand, which gives a definite place to passivity, openness, submission and non-action. And this non-action works miracles; this non-action is capable of results which ordinary action could never accomplish.

***

Swâmiji one day told me: "Inwardly, be actively passive; outwardly, be passively active." Just what is the meaning of this? "Inwardly be actively passive." Yet a certain amount of effort is required in order to be passive. Is there not something contradictory in this? Try to understand.

Because of conditions which are more or less common to all of us modern Westerners, we have got into the habit of repressing a large share of what our consciousness contains—part of our memories, part of our desires and fears—and all of this is bubbling up, from deep within our unconscious. Consequently, it is difficult for us to be silent when we want to be silent, to relax when we want to relax, to meditate when we want to meditate. This is because there are many diverse and contradictory tensions struggling within the unconscious or the subconscious, whose unrest and upheaval come up to the surface. Try to meditate: a succession of thoughts will come to distract you, to carry you away in one direction or another . . . fears, apprehensions, hopes, plus all those thoughts whose goal is to mask or to compensate for what we want to deny or what we have not accepted.

Physiological agitation adds to these thoughts. It is well-known that emotions end up destroying the body. All who have tried to meditate have discovered an irresistible desire to move, sometimes of almost comical intensity. The simple fact of asking ourselves to remain motionless gives rise to all sorts of unexpected itches, aches and pains which we do not usually feel, and we have great difficulty in remaining still.

Therefore, in order to be passive, non-active, silent, a certain activity is required because passivity will not come of itself. If you are a beginner in relaxation, for example, and you simply lie on your bed, your muscles will not really relax. If you actively ask your muscles to relax, if you direct your attention through each part of your body, convincing the muscles to relax more and more deeply, you will little by little obtain results. And this need for conscious intervention applies to all other aspects of agitation which manifest themselves when you try to remain inwardly silent. This should be well understood. You can contract a muscle by ordinary methods—that is not difficult. You can tighten your fist or clench your teeth. But you do not relax in the same manner. The effort is more subtle. Yet you cannot deeply relax your muscles unless you are active. If you are not active in the way you relax, you will daydream and those daydreams will be accompanied by various contractions. You must be vigilant, you must therefore be active in a certain way—but by relaxing, that is, being passive.

As soon as you return to the ordinary attitude, your muscles contract—either to run away from something, to take possession of what you desire, or to destroy. These are the three fundamental actions of man in his role as an animal: taking possession of what he covets (be it food or a female), running away if there is some danger which frightens him, and attacking to destroy his opponent. These three mechanisms involve a certain degree of contraction. And as long as the ego and the mind reign, it is these three fundamental ways of acting which reign over our existences. In actual practice, we know only these three drives. They are the source of all our behavior—from apparently lofty, refined, intellectual or esthetic levels down to coarser levels—at least as long as the religious dimension has not truly permeated our lives.

These three dynamisms being in a latent state within you, an effort of a new quality—a very new one—becomes necessary: the vigilance to relax. If your muscles are completely relaxed, you are no longer ready to seize, to take possession, to run away or to destroy. Muscular relaxation goes hand in hand with passivity, with submission and, from a certain point of view, with renunciation and abandon. When in danger, it is true that certain animals are capable of immediate and total muscular contraction. But an animal's subconscious is much less encumbered than yours.

Today man is left on his own; religion invariably no longer plays any more than a superficial role in his life. He can only rely on his own strength in order to live, satisfy his desires and protect himself against his fears. So you are always on the alert. You do not know the unconscious source of these tensions, but they are there. If you are totally relaxed physically, you accept for the moment not attempting to run away, to destroy or to seize.

Understand this point well: when muscles relax, deep inside they give up being tense, being ready for action, ready to seize, ready to attack, ready to react. Do you think that a woman who clenches her teeth and stiffens up, in order to better accomplish her task as procreator, will have a superior pregnancy? Definitely not! The less muscular tension a woman is under, *the less she feels the need to protect herself*, the more harmoniously natural laws will operate, and the more harmonious her pregnancy will also be.

Muscular relaxation is the easiest to understand and it is therefore the one to which we first have access. Then comes the relaxation of emotional and mental tensions which, for a long time, were expressed through religious belief—Christian, Moslem or Hindu—"I entrust myself entirely to God, I put my destiny into his hands, I trust Divine Providence. If certain trials come to me, I see in them the hand of God to purify me and to bring me closer to inner realization." Deep religious faith is a powerful factor of emotional relaxation. One feels less desire, less fear, for existence is seen in the light of a factor which most human beings today categorically push aside—one which has been called divine Grace, divine Providence, or God at work in the world.

We are also rarely relaxed mentally. We are continually on the go, thinking: you must do this, you must not do that, I should never have done this, why did he do that? If you try not to think according to your present state of consciousness—one of separation, limitation and vulnerability—you will see how difficult it is to remain open and silent. Yet those words, "open" and "silent," are the universal religious or spiritual language. I even came across the word "surrender": abandoning our prerogative of satisfying our needs or of protecting ourselves from danger and instead trusting a Life, a Force, superior to the limitation of our egocentric consciousness. Whether, like Swâmiji, you call it the Great Force of Universal Life, *Atma-Shakti,* or whether you call it God—that is just a question of vocabulary. But the common basis of all spiritual attitudes should be fully recognized. And that is not easy for you, as modern Westerners. You find letting go inwardly and opening yourselves much more difficult than acting by yourselves.

There are some who lift weights until they attain a muscular body. There are students who work nights in preparatory classes to get into top level teacher training school, Normale Supérieure or engineering school, Polytechnique. There are even men who pedal in the heat like the Tour de France's "giants of the road." But it is much less acceptable, much less tolerable, to discover the virtue of non-effort, of that female attitude which *allows*—collaborating while letting things happen.

In order to rediscover this passivity, we must be active in a certain way, one which should be well understood. "Inwardly, be actively passive." Otherwise you will remain ordinarily active— that is, tense, agitated and stiff. "Liberation" is first of all the complete relaxation of all tensions: physical, emotional and mental. And this does not happen by itself.

If we return to the example of muscular relaxation, you will realize that you are unable to relax your muscles in the same manner as you tense them, and yet they will not relax of their own accord. You can therefore be vigilant, in a certain active way: relax the forehead . . . a little bit more, the eyebrows, the jaws, the right shoulder, the left shoulder, the right wrist, the left wrist . . . relax . . . relax. This movement of relaxation is contrary to the habitual movement, because being relaxed is being vulnerable, it is refusing to be on the defensive, ready to act. The very principle of relaxation is to turn your back to muscular contraction, a contraction which gives us the safe feeling of being active.

You are afraid of this passive attitude. Mystical language—be it Sufi or Christian—is no longer appreciated. People smile at it or else they are shocked; everyone dreams of being the least passive possible. Men, women, everyone wants to be active. People consider themselves too passive—reading disillusionment, tiredness and lack of energy into the word. It is not at all the same thing—that must be clear. Let the word passive be associated in your mind with the word active (as the word inhaling is associated with the word exhaling, or the word day is associated with the word night), each word having equal value. And find more correct terms to describe states of weariness, discouragement, depression, tiredness, inability to put your heart into your work—all of which make you seek some remedy or simply look forward to a holiday or some rest.

As far as spirituality is concerned, it is passivity which truly prevails over activity. And understanding the value of passivity is what will save you, because ordinary activity has a limit. It comes from a state of mind called blindness, ignorance, sleep; it is not this activity which will lead you beyond the ego, or the "mind"—that mind which must be "destroyed." It can only be useful to you in order to eliminate false activity little by little, and to allow you to discover true passivity. Inwardly, be actively passive. Be sufficiently vigilant to push aside agitation, to overthrow the ordinary attitude, to bring about a conversion and to reunite yourself, in order to offer yourself to the action of a force much more vast than the limitation of the mind and the ego.

***

Outwardly, be passively active. Of course outwardly we are active, but there is a relaxed way of being active, without tension. You could compare it to an actor who is playing a role on stage. Outwardly, the actor can be very active. The role of Cyrano de Bergerac, for example, is reserved for athletes—at the end of the play, the actor comes off stage "wiped out." But an actor can play the entire role of Cyrano, bring the audience to tears, and perhaps cry a few tears himself, while remaining inwardly absolutely re-

laxed, because his own ego is not concerned. He knows that he is
not going to die of a head wound at the end of the fifth act. On stage,
he is an "actor"—one who acts. But inwardly he is silent, at ease,
submitting to his role and to the setting.

This is what is also required of you: to be apparently active
(perhaps even very active) but passively active. Certain sages were
apparently much more active than contemplative, like Buddha who,
until the age of eighty, traveled across Bihar and the North of India,
or Shânkarachârya who covered all of India even though he died
quite young. Mâ Anandamayì also proved to be very active, even
in her old age. Be inwardly passive, without tension, open to become
the instrument of an understanding, an intelligence, a vision, an
energy other than your usual capacities. Cosmic energy and intelligence are limited in us, retracted, like a section within Immen-
sity. You will only progress if you open yourself to these ideas, if
you feel their truth.

Ramana Maharshi said, "There are only two methods—either
to practice the search for the Self (the non-religious method, the
Vedantic method, the metaphysical method) or else *surrender*." This
word, so often used in India, means letting go, abandoning the ego
and putting complete trust in Providence—a trust which you will
never take back again. If you are sick, your trust in Providence must
not immediately disappear. Agree to be sick, but recognize that it
is also Providence that sends a doctor or that permits you to meet
one. If you follow the fundamental religious attitude through to
the end, one can also attain the egoless state. It was not the way
specifically taught by Ramana Maharshi, but it is one whose value
he never ceased to publicly recognize.

The direct Vedantic way toward discovery of the Self is also
a way of silence. Thought is effaced little by little, tensions disappear, the "root" thought—I am me—is suspended, and infinite
Consciousness is revealed. But, do not be mistaken, we cannot force
it to be revealed. Although powerful and even surprising spiritual
disciplines have been taught, all masters—all of them—are unanimous in affirming that these are only preparation; we will still have
to *open ourselves* to that divine, metaphysical, unlimited, infinite
Reality which our ego can neither imagine nor conquer.

Preparatory spiritual discipline purifies the ego, makes the mind flexible, allows us to neutralize the powerful dynamisms of the great fears and the great desires which bring us back to ordinary action. At times, certain ascetics have used heroic methods. And after all, Christ did say "the violent will take the Kingdom of Heaven by force." You can use certain energetic methods to prepare yourself, to push to their limit the desires and fears which constitute your deep nature, and to push to their limit the three dynamisms (seizing what attracts you, and destroying or running away from what repulses you). Dangerous ascetic practices do exist—not to mention more or less risky modern experimental methods and, even worse, certain contemporary extravagances sold on the world market in the name of Hinduism or Buddhism.

Inwardly, be actively passive; outwardly, be passively active. This brings about a shift, a reversal of the usual attitude. The ego knows only itself. It has no proof that a divine force can come to its aid, and it wants to solve everything on its own, through ordinary effort. But of course the other side of ordinary effort is ordinary passivity, weariness, tiredness, depression, when everything feels so heavy, when nothing any longer appeals. You cannot dissociate the couple activity-passivity. If you are active in the ordinary manner (and 99% of human beings in the West are active in the ordinary manner) then it is the ego which is active, having confidence only in itself, and keeping you tensely aiming for a goal. And the other face of this is discouragement, when it is not utter dejection.

You cannot remain constantly active in the ordinary sense of the word. But if you can harmoniously balance activity and passivity, you will no longer feel those cyclical movements of elation and depression . . . when one day everything seems possible and, one week later, you are in the depths of discouragement. If inwardly you are actively passive and outwardly you are passively active, you will be able to remain constant whether the weather is warm or cold, whether there is a lot of work or hardly any, whether all goes well or everything goes wrong. You will no longer be subjected to inner states of change over which you have absolutely no power. You will attain stability.

***

As long as you only know the individualized state of consciousness—*ahamkara* or ego—and the manner of vision and understanding which we call "mind," it is difficult to understand what I am trying to say now. I will go further and say that the conscious or unconscious goal of every human being is to suppress duality. Yes. You will see that this is not really complicated. "Duality" means that there are two—that is all. And the essential duality for us is the duality: me—that which is not me. When we incarnate, we establish ourselves in duality. A separate little fragment appears in the All, taking the form of an egg and a sperm in fusion. Here therefore is a being with civil status, termed as a "person" in law. And we have only one goal—to put an end to this duality—because we are governed by the law of attraction and repulsion.

We cannot accept being separated from that which attracts us. We want to join it to ourselves in one way or another, to make it ours. If a man is in love with a woman, he feels the duality: "I exist, this woman exists; she attracts me, I am in love with her; I cannot be happy if she escapes me, if I never see her again or if she marries someone else; therefore I will try to join her to myself." And perhaps "if all goes well," that man and woman will be united by the bond of marriage. United means made one.

Then, education makes us reduce our claims. We know that we cannot enter a store and take what we please. We must pay. All of existence is based on such simple truths. Duality is our state of consciousness, yet we do not want duality. If we feel attracted to something, we want to unite it to ourselves, and since there then exists only one, we have eliminated the duality.

We want to annihilate what repulses us; the duality will then also be eliminated, because one of the two terms of the duality will have disappeared. For that other term of the duality to disappear, there are two possibilities: either destroy it (it will no longer exist) or run away from it. Sometimes a man, too deeply in love with a woman who has just married one of his friends, goes off to Hong Kong or Australia to put the greatest possible distance between himself and the woman. Distance diminishes suffering. It is also well-known that in a crime of passion, a man destroys—kills—the woman whom he has begged to marry him, to whom he has said "I love you" for the last time just one hour before.

These are the three fundamental mechanisms to which you are subjected. They are constantly at work. If a science interests you, you get rid of the duality between yourself and whatever you are studying. You do not want that subject to be on one side while you are on the other, so you attempt to attain non-duality with it in the form of scientific study.

You will not find any activity—except that of someone committed to a spiritual path—which does not enter into one of these three categories, having this elimination of duality through ordinary, known means as its goal (although that goal may be more or less obvious or masked). Duality means ego-consciousness or mind-functioning . . . a non-objective, egocentric vision of the world. And this is what you want to escape. But how are you going to do it?

Unless there is a new understanding, you will assimilate what you call the Path, the Way, Yoga, Spiritual Life with the activities you already know. You may choose to call it Awakening, Wisdom, Liberation, purification of the psychism or destruction of the mind, and you establish a certain goal for yourself. You feel separated from this goal and want to "attain" it—therefore to be united with it. For a senior in high school, the title "high school graduate" is still a separate reality. There is a duality. The day he becomes a high school graduate, he attains non-duality. He and the title "high school graduate" coincide. However the same kind of effort that helped you obtain the title "high school graduate" will not help you obtain the title "Sage" or "Liberated One." You must also be perfectly aware of that. If you are not very vigilant, you will turn toward your "spiritual" goals with the ordinary mentality, believing that ordinary methods can succeed. You will continue to be active in the wrong way, with moments of passivity. At times you will decide: "Now I am going to put the teachings into practice. I will get up early, do yoga, fast, stop smoking, meditate—I will be one with all that presents itself." Then sooner or later, these fervent outbursts are squashed, the pendulum swings the other way, discouragement inevitably takes over and the teachings no longer even interest you. Once again, some stimulant appears—a meeting with a Tibetan sage, for example—and under the shock of the sage's presence, the movement again reverses and again you decide "now things will start happening; I am going to commit myself to the Way."

If you have been interested in spiritual life for some years now, all of this will perhaps strike an echo in you. You recognize all the desires which make up your overall desire for liberation and, on the other hand, there is either weariness and discouragement, a new amorous infatuation, an improvement in your job situation or some profane accomplishment in the world of form. Left to your own devices, using the methods you know, even though you be gifted with courage, intelligence and perseverance, you will still remain, and still function, within the ego and the mind.

In India or other spiritualized civilizations, pregnancy was praised to the skies. A pregnant woman, simply because she is pregnant, is considered to represent the Goddess--the *Devi*, the *Shakti*. She is helped to be actively passive—ever more passive, ever more open, ever more available, ever more silent, ever more centered in herself—in order to collaborate in a task which surpasses her. This is the religious attitude—to be actively passive in order to collaborate in a task which surpasses us. That task can be called the grace of God or the revelation of the Atman, but no ordinary means will open the door for you to the Kingdom of Heaven or to the realization of the Self.

Fundamentally, this is not only the religious orientation, it is also the metaphysical orientation. It is written in the Upanishads: "The Atman is revealed to those to whom it wishes to be revealed." What you can do is put yourself into this attitude of openness and remain there. You can learn, through your efforts and through your sadhana, to become truly passive, actively passive, open. Then this Force, this Reality, this Life—which has possibilities that your ego and your mind will never have—will start to manifest through you, to animate you and even to direct your actions. You will discover in yourself an intelligence which you did not suspect until now, allowing you to appreciate a situation, to appreciate the truth of a moment, like a new vision. It is sometimes said that the scales have fallen from our eyes, the deforming lenses which blurred our vision have disappeared, or the blind see, the deaf hear, the paralyzed walk. Christ's miracles can be taken literally, but they can also be taken symbolically, as images of this transformation.

Remember the famous words of St. Paul: "It is no longer I who lives but Christ who lives in me" or "Not I, but Christ lives in me." These words have universal value. It is no longer I as an ego who lives, it is the *Shakti* who lives in me; it is Buddhahood, the Buddha state, which lives in me; it is Divine Life, Supreme Energy.

You cannot be stronger, more intelligent, more cunning than this necessity to drop effort and to simply become an instrument. It is a fundamental step in all spiritual ways, even those where courage, energy and determination (therefore apparently activity and effort) play a visible role. This new understanding must permeate each detail of your practice from the present moment on. It is not simply a key which is given to you for one day in the future when you will be ready to let go. Inwardly be actively passive. Outwardly be passively active. Therefore in both cases, be relaxed.

Can you relax all tensions? You know how to relax physically. A muscle cannot be relaxed in the same manner as it can be contracted; it is not the same mechanism. How can you be actively passive, yet passive? Meditation is absolute non-effort. This is the truth. However you are constantly in a state of effort to stop what is deep within from coming up to the surface, in order to continue repressing, suppressing, censoring. And it is this very resistance which must be put aside. But although what is deep inside cannot be forced to express itself, what stops us from expressing ourselves can be acted upon. For this, a certain skill has to be developed. Some discover it very quickly, even immediately, while others take much more time and continue struggling to try to unite the surface and the depths.

Here it is not a question of effort. The secret of non-effort must be discovered through vigilance, so every attempt to be silent is precious. Let go, try to let go, to no longer act, to let things happen. At first, it is not the Atman which will reveal itself, but rather your buried fears, your unconsoled sadnesses, your unaccomplished desires. But this is the Way which will one day lead you, in the same manner, through this inner silence, to your welcome into Infinity. It is a case of a very particular effort. Search until you find its secret. This effort of non-effort consists in making you actively non-active so that something can be accomplished which can only be accomplished in abandon, in letting go, in confidence, in submission, in openness.

Outwardly, what is non-action? You must first discover the most quickly understandable manner for you to act in a relaxed way, without tension. "I will do what I can do; I will do what the circumstances require." This is always submission . . . submission to the necessity of those situations, to the necessity of those conditions, which are yours.

Circumstances arise—ones over which you have only very limited control (if indeed we admit that you do have some control). Responding to circumstances first of all involves submitting to them, in order to provide the right and corresponding response. Thereafter, you can be active. You can make a telephone call, write a letter, perhaps speak firmly and severely, perhaps even show anger while inwardly remaining as neutral and relaxed as an actor on stage, acting in appearance like one who is involved although you are completely detached inside.

***

But there is more. There is that which truly religious people know, and it is true; it is therefore also true for a way like the Vedanta which has an apparently non-religious form. Deeply religious people know that if they are non-active, but in a vigilant manner, that which they themselves were unable to accomplish can be accomplished. In ordinary religious language, this is called putting one's problem into the hands of God . . . praying. Oh! These are words we all know. I realize that those words are suspicious for quite a few of you—because they are associated with bad memories. Yet because there are many disappointing aspects in today's Catholicism and Protestantism, do not reject the truth of spirituality at the same time as you reject a Christianity which

disappointed you, or a religious mentality which seems to be il-
lustrated only by bigots and priests lost in their own problems. Truth
itself will always be truth. For one who has the religious attitude
and who—unified—offers his problem to God, there are so many
"miracles," so many accomplishments that take place in vigilant
non-action, in silently active non-action.

We think, discuss, try to act, try to "do" . . . and we fail, we
get nowhere. If you were capable of being totally silent, "I will not
try anything more. It is beyond my power. Let God act," then you
would be surprised to see the result you wished for come about.

Two examples come to mind. My son, who was ten years old
at the time, experienced the founding of my first ashram, the Bost,
as what is considered a tragic trauma. He had always lived with
me, as conditions had allowed me to take him along on all my
voyages. And then suddenly, his father disappeared from his
existence; at the same time, he caught a case of viral hepatitis which
made him even more vulnerable. He came to the Bost for a few days
but things went very badly. His mother was in Paris. There was
only Josette to help me, but she was in the hospital at the time. An
elderly lady who had a decided tendency to dictate, due to enthusiasm and good will, had said to the child: "Do you think that this
is your home? You are in an ashram! Your home is in Paris." Those
words were unbearable for that little boy.

It must have been eight or eight-thirty in the evening when I
was finally free to spend time with him. He had locked himself into
a bedroom and slid a note for me under the door. It said, "I will
not open the door until I die, I am so sad and unhappy." I tried,
"Listen to me, Emmanuel!" No answer. "Come on, open the door."
No answer. "But listen, at least we can talk." A few minutes later,
I heard: "Look at the note I put under the door." I replied, "But I
read the note." Once again, silence. It could have seemed terrible.
If, first of all, I had not been one with the situation (cruel as it
sounds), if there had been any emotion, things would have been
worse. But feeling gave me the heart's understanding of the suffering of that child locked in the room; I felt how wounded he was.
I sat down on the other side of the door. That was all. And I did
nothing. No talk, no argument. Nothing. I sat down to be intensely

silent, passive, actively passive. In Christian language, I "offered the situation to God" (this is the problem, this is my limit, here I am incapable; it is Your turn to act). I was silent, totally non-active, without any thoughts . . . simply vigilant, as if in a state of formless prayer or meditation, in nothing but submission and love. And after a while, I heard the key turn in the lock. Therefore the door was no longer locked. I remained silent—I did not open it. And a few minutes later, the little boy opened the door. I will not tell you about the rest of the evening. I had to be passively active, very active, for two, three, four years in order to cure the wound of that son who was so ill-at-ease, so unhappy, that he became demanding and capricious—like every child who is suffering.

Another example comes to mind—that of a man whose karma was very heavy. He was a person who had accumulated sufferings since childhood, and had very great difficulty accepting our ashram, once he had put his hopes in it. He tried "lyings" to purify the unconscious, and, having reached deadlock, he lived in a state of ambivalence, of hope and bitterness toward me. I tried one method; I tried another. I spoke to him in one way; I spoke to him in another. Without results. So one morning when he came into the room, and lay down for his "lying," I did nothing . . . nothing. An almost unbearable tension emanated from him. I did nothing except remain in a state of prayer, silence, and non-action . . . actively passive. He was lying there—tense, torn, in pain—but I felt that what was emanating from him was less violent. Little by little, a relaxation spread over him; he began to cry. The tears flowed; he was reunified. He began to sob, he took me by the hand, I clasped him in my arms, and then he left. I had not said one word. Non-acting had accomplished that which action (even inwardly passive action, without the egocentric desire to succeed) had not obtained.

Spiritual life starts when we become instruments of a Reality, a Life, an Energy, far superior in all respects to our usual functionings . . . even to our efficiency, intelligence or knowledge. It is no longer I who acts, it is Wisdom which acts through me. In India, this is primarily what is called the egoless state. Ramdas said: "Be an instrument, but a conscious instrument, not like a pen, unconscious of what is being written through it."

Even more so than others, Ramdas was eloquent in describing non-effort. I was once present when he told this little story: Vishnu and Lakshmi (his understudy) were together in Paradise. Vishnu suddenly left, saying: "My servant Haridas has been attacked by brigands; I am going to his rescue." One second later, Vishnu returned. Lakshmi was surprised: "Already?"

"Yes, Haridas had just bent down to pick up a stone." That was the end of the story. "If Haridas was picking up a stone, then he intended to defend himself on his own and he therefore had no need of Me." This effectively explains why, when you read Ramdas's *In Quest of God*, you have the impression that he did not even try to take care of himself when he was sick. He counted on Ram to make him better. And indeed, each time Ram sent him people who felt compassion for this sâdhu shivering with fever, and took care of him. It is a book to read—so original and so convincing.

I did not feel that I was ready not to pick up stones if brigands attacked me in the forest. I did not feel ready for such letting go. But I have never been able to erase the impact those words of Ramdas had on me. And it was with Swâmiji that I was able to harmonize activity and passivity, the male attitude and the female attitude, action and non-action. Ordinary effort—which, for a long time, is the only kind you know—will not take you far. How can you become inwardly actively passive? In relation to the Great Reality (call it God, Shakti or Brahman), how can you have a female attitude and let yourself be impregnated, as the Virgin Mary let herself be impregnated by the Holy Spirit? Be actively collaborators of this force, which is so much bigger, more intelligent, more "right" than your ego or your mind. Act in a relaxed way—physically relaxed, emotionally relaxed, mentally relaxed—as an instrument of what Swâmiji described as "what the situation merits," of what others call "God's will" until you discover that a unique Infinite Energy, *Atma-Shakti*, is acting everywhere. Rediscover your identity, your communion, with this Unique Energy.

7

MARRIAGE

Who, at some moment of his life or even at various times during his existence, from adolescence to maturity, has not dreamed of true love? And who has not thought he had found it or tried to live with someone, hoping it would work out and perhaps putting great expectations into it?

Furthermore it must be stated that marriage is considered sacred in all traditions. For those who have the smallest notion of what Christianity is, the word sacrament is very strong; it is not a case of a simple benediction. From the theological point of view, this shows the importance that, in the past, religious thought gave to the union of man and woman. In India, the rite of marriage is also essential, and the wife plays a very important role in the couple; she is, in certain respects, the priestess of the home.

Today, the casual manner in which people marry, separate, live together while unmarried, change partners and divorce shows that we live in a world which is what it is, but which we cannot consider to be the norm of human behavior. In any case, we should recognize that it goes against what has been lived in all civilizations until now. If you wish, you can consider this progress—that is a matter of how you interpret it. But since the fact cannot be questioned, we should at least see that it is a case of a very specific mentality. Yet this is the mentality with which we are impregnated. It is also the one against which many young people are starting to react.

Part of what Swâmiji transmitted to me in this regard is already contained in the second volume of *Ways of Wisdom*, in the chapter entitled "Make Love," which concerns not only sexuality, but also the couple and marriage.

There is one question that comes up before all others, once we think we have found the ideal partner and are considering marriage: "How can we be sure that we are not making a mistake?"

111

It is a question I have often been asked over the past ten years. As long as we are carried away with passion, we ask no questions—but the time comes when this fascination can no longer hide the doubts which arise. "Have I made a mistake? Have I really found the one of whom I have always been dreaming? Are we made for each other?" How can one answer these questions?

Certainly not through emotions, the fascination of love, or the prejudices of our present society. According to Swâmiji, there are five criteria which allow one to know if two people are "made for each other" and if their union will lead them to happiness. Otherwise there will be suffering, quarrels and reconciliations . . . those agitated, wounded, painful loves which last because one has not got the courage to end them, and which bring nothing of that to which one who embarks upon the Way of Wisdom aspires: inner peace, serenity and stability, the possibility to fulfill oneself and the possibility to truly commune.

This communion, which is the culmination of love or of the couple, establishes itself over the years. An ardent, brief love affair—like one you see in certain films or novels—is not to be confused with marriage. Allow me to use the word "marriage," even if today people marry less and less frequently. Already people no longer marry in church, and abolishing marriage at the City Hall is considered from time to time in "higher circles." That would leave only certain notarized contracts. I will use the word "marriage" even though it may make me appear retrograde and reactionary.

"They will be but one soul and one body." Those words should not be taken lightly. "One soul and one body" . . . this is no ordinary accomplishment. And the fascination of love never leads to this veritable communion; it creates an illusion of non-duality which maintains separation. If this state of non-duality, of real communion, of being one with each other, can be established between a man and a woman, the marriage has been consecrated by a sacrament. In the past, there was royal ordination and priestly ordination; now we can also speak of conjugal ordination. From the point of view of the Way of Wisdom, of the discovery of the Self and of Ultimate Consciousness—a couple relationship is destined to last. An intense love in brief and exceptional conditions can be a theme for an admirable film, but it is not in itself a path leading toward the purification of the emotions and the effacing of the ego. Marriage is a way toward the destruction of the mind and the purification of the psychism.

Swâmiji therefore one day put forth for me five criteria by which we can recognize the deep value of a couple. I have often thought about them. It is astonishing that in those five criteria, the word "love" is not to be found. That surprised me at first. Then I remembered that Swâmiji only used the word "love" with great gravity. In French, we use the word "love" left and right, if I may say so. But Swâmiji preferred to say "sympathy" or "compassion;" he only used the word "love" when I was worthy of hearing it— like a word one has no right to pronounce unless one gives it its true sense. How often we use the word "love" for that which is simply emotion or attraction . . . and attraction always includes its counter aspect—the possibility to detest that which we adored a moment before.

***

The first of these criteria is *"a feeling of companionship."* Indeed in French we sometimes say "my companion." And we can ask ourselves: is there the feeling that I am no longer alone? To have a companion is to no longer feel alone.

However I think you will agree with me that many married men and women—or men and women who live as if they were married—still feel alone. During the last ten years, I have become used to hearing the heartfelt cry of one or another of you, and I have heard "I am alone," "I have always been alone" spring from the heart of married men and women, or from those who on the contrary have lived various intense loves during their lives. The suffering of this solitude, which can be rooted in childhood, is not effaced by a love relationship. The attraction of love, of course, is that it is the hope of no longer feeling alone; it is the illusion of no longer feeling alone. Will it last? That is the question.

What I want to talk about today always concerns a length of time, a way to follow together. *"To grow together"*—to blossom together, to progress together on the path of maturity and fullness, without the petty and childish emotions of the ego coming to corrupt, whittle down and diminish existence.

"A feeling of companionship "—the feeling of no longer being alone, of having a real companion. Our husband or wife should also be our best friend. The wife should be able to play all the roles for the husband that a woman can play for a man, and the husband should be able to play for his wife all the roles a man can play for a woman. The man, or the woman, feels fulfilled and does not feel the nostalgia to find elsewhere that which he or she no longer lacks. Can I consider my husband or my wife to be my best friend? It is a simple question. The word "love" does not come into it . . . that word "love" which dupes and deceives you so!

Indeed you will notice that friendship does not wear out over the years. It happens that life separates us from a friend or that our interests diverge. But most often, he or she who was our best friend when we were twenty is still our best friend when we are seventy. We remember having shared a happy or difficult moment, we have a common language, a deep complicity. Why, in this modern world, are there indestructible friendships, without our having to make any special effort of fidelity—and yet so many loves wear out, and after two or three years we start looking around again and taking an interest in other men, in other women?

If this feeling of having found a real companion exists, it is enriched over the years with shared experiences, with memories . . . it never stops enriching itself, as opposed to the ordinary passion of love, condemned to lose its intensity like a fire that consumes itself and goes out.

The second criterion is even simpler: *"at-ease-ness."* It is interesting to see that the word "disease" means sickness, and that "at ease" also concerns perfect health. You do not hurt anywhere; you feel well. *"At-ease-ness"* is feeling perfectly well; everything is easy. But too often, in the fascination of love there is wonder and there are intense moments, "divine" moments—otherwise love's fascination would not be so powerful—but there is neither ease nor facility. Those words, when pronounced by Swâmiji in his little ashram in Bengal, had a powerful resonance in me because I felt how little I had known such relaxation—except as a youth of twenty-four, during my engagement, which was later to be broken by a grave case of pulmonary tuberculosis. Apart from that engagement, which was as peaceful as possible but which life destroyed, I had to recognize that, in the different loves in which I had believed, there had been outbursts, tears, misunderstandings, supplications, quarrels, reconciliations, diverse misfortunes, but not that simple *"at-ease-ness."*

I often meet one or another of the partners of a couple, whose talk with me is essentially concerned with their husband-wife relationship, and who are at the antipodes of this facility, this ease. "I love him, but he makes me suffer!"; "I love her but she tortures me"; "I love her but I have reached the end of my rope"; "I love him but I cannot take any more . . . " How can you consider that such a relationship—however stimulating or intense it may be—can prove the phrase: "They will be but one soul and one body" . . . true communion, surpassing the limitation of the ego, plenitude?

Or else a certain ease is established in the relationship—but it is established in routine, in monotony, and the heart feels that something is missing. This is not what you dreamed of as an adolescent, and you remain susceptible to a new case of love at first sight—against which you will struggle more or less—depending on if you are more or less marked by a religious upbringing, or more or less stirred by maternal or paternal instinct and put the children's interests before your own.

We therefore already have the first two criteria: *"A feeling of companionship"*: I am not alone; there is someone by my side who understands me, with whom I like to communicate, with whom I like to share, with whom I like to act, to do things together.

And *"at-ease-ness"*: an easy relationship that does not bring me to waste a large amount of my energy in emotions, and that does not oblige me to struggle against emotions.

When one is in love, one is inclined to say: "Forever . . . it is forever," or even: "We knew each other in all of our past lives, and we will find each other again in all our future lives" or "We will be united for all eternity." That "forever"—is it a word which corresponds to reality?

The third criterion: "*Two natures which are not too different.*" It is so simple, but for me the value of these criteria is that they are so simple I never would have thought of them, and for at least fifteen years I have been constantly confirming their value.

"*Two natures which are not too different.*" There is, in that, a point which is obviously fundamental. It is normal that there be a difference and a complementary aspect between a man and a woman. We will never find our alter-ego, a double of ourselves who, at each instant, is simply the incarnation of our projection of the moment. We will never find a spouse who is always exactly what we want, who is always in the mood or state of mind that we would like, who utters just the words we have been waiting for—never. And we must realize that. It is a childish demand, unworthy of an adult and destructive of any effort to build a couple, to want one's spouse to be no more than the support for one's projections and to respond at each moment to that which we demand, mechanically, through our ego and our emotion. This is an illusion which you should succeed in eradicating through awareness and through vigilance. The other is another. And even if this communion of "only one soul and only one body" is established, the other will never have our unconscious, our *samskaras*, our *vasanas*, our heredity. There will always be a difference.

It can be noted that, in a true couple, a deeper and deeper communication is established down through the years—especially if they share everything and if they really live together—to the point that one almost manages to read the other's thoughts. And perhaps you have noticed that after a long conjugal life, it has happened that a man and a woman end up looking alike, thinking together and feeling things together . . . their differences diminish little by little and each one expands to the dimension of the other and becomes enriched with the other's possibilities of understanding. But such a road is long, and it is quite a different matter from an intensive amorous passion—perhaps blinding and unforgettable, but brief.

"*Two natures which are not too different.*" Yet the fascination of love takes no account of this criterion. The unconscious of one reacts to, and on, the unconscious of the other; a facial trait, a smile, a hairstyle or a look touches an imprint in the depths of our psychism—and we are attracted. It even happens that a man can discover his father in a woman and a woman can discover her mother in a man. For the unconscious, one detail can become all-powerful: simply a look, for example. Leaving aside the rest of the face, the eyes effectively have nothing that is specifically male or female.

Therefore, the unconscious is suddenly fascinated by an appearance or an attitude and, if this mechanism is reciprocal, two people who are attracted to each other consider themselves to be in love. But if their natures are too different, no life together is possible, and their love will be utterly defeated by reality. Extreme cases of this will seem obvious. If a man is rather solitary, likes long walks in the country and the outdoor life, while a woman dreams only of fashionable gatherings, brilliant dinner parties and receptions, then their natures are too different. And still that will not stop them from falling in love.

Two natures which are not different—this does not exist. "Two natures which are not *too* different." And now I understand to what extent I was attracted by women whose natures were so different from mine that an understanding was beyond our respective capacities. One would have to be much more advanced along the Way to inner freedom to be capable of forming a peaceful couple with a partner whose nature is radically different from our own. Abandon the childish demand that your "soulmate" will be yourself in every way. One day you will come home from work very happy: "I am late because I went to the Metropolitan Opera and bought two tickets for tonight's concert." And your true love, instead of exclaiming: "Wonderful!" will answer: "Oh no, not tonight. I really do not want to go out." "What!" Ah yes. When you believe yourself to be very much in love, it happens that a little, insignificant incident like that wounds you. "I have made a mistake. She is not 'the one.' We are not made for each other." What childishness—but it is unfortunately true. In the first place, I experienced it myself in the past, and in addition I see reality quite clearly now that my existence has led me to share the secrets—sometimes the most hidden ones—of the hearts and intimate lives of others.

Do not forget this truth: the fascination of love superbly ignores the incompatibility of two natures. You honestly think you are in love—but there is no possibility of real understanding. You cannot fit together two mechanical parts which do not correspond. The complementary state of a man and a woman is based on difference, but it is also based on the possibility of association, of fitting together, of complicity.

Fourth criterion: *"Complete trust and confidence."* Trust is the perfection of confidence. Does this confidence exist? Those who ask themselves if they are made for each other can ask themselves: "Do I feel this complete confidence within myself? Has this man, this woman, been able to inspire such confidence in me?" I wonder if I have seen one true example of this. I see couples where the man does not really have confidence in his wife, nor the woman in her husband. There is no confidence because there is fear. Have the courage to see it and realize that no durable love—capable of growing and blossoming—is possible on such a foundation.

Of course, many men and women today have been wounded to the very depths of their unconscious by past betrayals—ones which prove to be much older than this present life and which they have brought with them at birth, or betrayals experienced at the age of two months or six months. Swâmiji told me of the case of one of his old disciples who lived in an uneasiness whose origin was apparently insignificant. As a baby, when this Indian was nursing, he bit his mother's nipple and she brusquely tore him away and hit him. And that baby, who until then had only known the bliss of maternal love and the joy of his mother's breast—his supreme happiness—was so traumatized that the adult thereafter lived in the unconscious fear of betrayal.

That sort of wound very often exists in your unconscious and it does not facilitate communion, an open approach, the mutual giving of oneself in love. That is why this criterion is so important.

Has this woman been able to inspire real confidence in me? Deep inside, I feel that she can make mistakes, she can be wrong, she can even do something which creates a momentary difficulty for me, one I will have to resolve . . . but she cannot hurt me.

Basically, it is this certainty which prevails.

And Swâmiji's words are very strong: *"Complete trust and confidence."* There is an old French expression which says: "I swear by my trust"; it comes from the language of lovers. The word "trust" holds a density, a richness, a graveness. There is a religious aspect to love.

Marriage cannot be a spiritual way towards wisdom if this confidence and this trust do not exist, if you are living in fear. You will have to be stronger than your childishness and not destroy a precious relationship yourself through completely unjustified mistrust. The partners must no longer be totally childish; they must have a certain understanding of their own mechanisms, decide to go beyond them and to be more adult. Even if you are very much in love with your companion, the great love of your life, you can see her talking with another man during a reception, look at him in a certain way, perhaps even take him aside to talk more quietly— if you are spending the evening at the house of friends and there are a lot of guests—without feeling a fear arise inside: "What is going on? What are they talking about?" It is only this complete confidence that eliminates the poison of love . . . jealousy.

It is indeed rare that one who is in love be free from jealousy. I am not saying that it is a vice or a sin; it is a particularly childish emotion in which the mind invents something for which it has no proof. Nothing is more destructive of love than such jealousy. A woman whose husband is jealous no longer feels respected. In the usual dialectics of love, there is something flattering in this jealousy: "As long as she is jealous, it means that I am the best, that I have her; the day she no longer minds if I court another woman, I will have lost my power over her." But in the couple on a spiritual way, jealousy cannot have any place.

The last criterion: *"A strong impulse to make the other happy."* This is not as easy as it seems. And it also demands an adult approach to the couple. The demand to be happy because of another is natural, normal, legitimate in a man or a woman who has not reached the end of the Way and whose happiness is not yet purely an expression of Being, who still feels incomplete. It is the other, as I see him through my projections and my own demands, that I am trying to make happy by offering him what I want to offer him, by doing for her what I feel like doing, and without considering his or her real demands. The confidences of my fellow man have often led me to emphasize this criterion.

Wanting to make another happy is still situated in the duality of myself and others—others and myself. It means considering that others expect something of me, that we have not yet established the perfect communion of Being, beyond all question of "having." Each one expects happiness from the other. But that happiness is also a simple daily reality, composed of an accumulation of little details, and not only of hearing "I love you" from the one we love.

Swâmiji said: *"There is no giving without receiving."* If you give and yet the other has not received, it is as though you had not given. If you do not give what the other expects, consciously or unconsciously—if you do not give what is necessary to him—then you have not given to him. Imagine a purely carnivorous animal to which you feed only lettuce (as if it were a rabbit); you have given it nothing and it will die of hunger. Imagine that you bring the best cuts of meat to a rabbit; you have given it nothing and it will die of hunger. This simple image makes you smile, but for me it crudely and clearly illustrates that which I have too often witnessed.

How many parents affirm from the bottom of their hearts: "But I have lived only for my children . . . I have sacrificed myself to them . . . I have given them everything . . . " And the children sob: "I have received nothing." It is the cry of frustration; at times it pours out from their very depths like the cry of the heart. There is no giving without receiving. It is true for the relationship of parents with their children; it is true for all human relationships. And it is true for that which concerns us today—the couple.

Giving is not giving that which *we* want to give, to a partner as *we* want him to be, but rather to a partner as he is and as we must learn to see him, to understand him and to feel him. Here intervenes that intelligence of the heart which the emotions veil. If in a couple there is not that feeling of being two companions, two real friends . . . if there is not that complete confidence, that facility, that ease . . . if the natures are too different and there are stormy situations . . . if, in a word, there are too many emotions, then the intelligence of the heart is blinded. You think you have done much for your wife, for your husband—and the other has not received. What rending, what suffering!

I have heard wives explain to me all the sacrifices they had made for their husbands-and from their point of view, this was unquestionable. As for the husband, he felt but regret and disappointment. And on the other hand, I have heard men describe to me all they had done for their wives, and the wife felt only frustration and was still looking for the true love of whom she had been dreaming since she was sixteen.

There is no giving without receiving; we cannot feel what the other truly needs unless the intelligence of the heart has been awakened.

There are so many marriages in which that impulse to make the other happy has disappeared. It is a motivation, an animation which is dead. You do not want to hurt "her," but you have lost— or never had—the ability to feel what can make her happy: what gesture you can make, what word you can say, what decision you can make, what activity you can organize, what gift you can offer. This desire to make the other happy cannot be artificially fabricated; it is there or it is not there. The other as *himself,* I insist on that point. "What! I gave her a marvelous ring!" Yes, you wanted to give her a luxurious present and, in the passion of love, you gave her a ring that corresponds to a drive from your own unconscious. And if your unconscious had been different, instead of a ring you would have given her a violin. That will not stop the cry of frustration I have too often heard—but the accumulation of little gifts, little gestures will. A person needs to breathe every instant, and he needs to breathe love every day.

"A strong impulse to make the other happy" is a permanent feeling, like that which a mother feels for her child when it is still young and dependent: "I exist for him; what can I do for him?" This intelligence of the heart would awaken very naturally in you if your emotions did not corrupt the possibility of true feeling.

***

These criteria are simple. But if they are put together, believe me, all else follows, including sexual harmony. Before giving details on this point, I wish to repeat—so that it will be clear in your mind—that I am speaking today of a durable couple, not of that great amorous passion which illuminates life for an instant but does not resist the passing years. I am speaking of the "eternal love" which lovers swear to each other and which life almost always belies, leading either to separation or to a worn out, bleak, poor relationship that will never be a way towards the Kingdom of Heaven within ourselves and towards supreme Wisdom.

We can consider that the criterion "two natures which are not too different" includes the sexual criterion, at least in part. The book of "kama sutras" (sold with a very humorous label because it always says "expurgated edition") is not simply a description of the different sexual positions. It is a voluminous treatise on the couple and marriage, written by a very great Indian sage. And from this is extracted, or was extracted (when sex shops, which have since done even more in that line, did not yet exist), a chapter which describes the positions of the sexual act. This edition—expurgated indeed, but expurgated of all philosophy—was sold by the book vendors along the Seine River in Paris. And the characteristic of these kama sutras was that, in marriages fixed by family gurus and astrologers, they gave instructions on the way to predict if the two adolescents who were to be married would get along well sexually or not.

Here also, there is a point to which I should make a quick reference when speaking of the couple. It is an element that has given me much reflection. Whatever my goodwill in regard to the Hindu tradition, my intelligence as an educated Westerner (or my stupidity, call it as you wish) made this aspect—so shocking for us—impossible for me to understand. "How can a man and a woman be happy together when they have not chosen each other freely?"

I even remember the period when I watched Hindu women in the street while thinking about this and asking myself about women I did not find at all attractive: "What if I had been married to this one? And what if I had been married to that one?" I was hindered by such simple reactions and as often as I went back over it during my talks with Swâmiji, I still did not understand because Swâmiji persisted imperturbably in affirming that, for centuries and centuries, it had given very satisfactory results. Indeed, I personally knew a number of Indian couples who, at the age of fifty or sixty, made one feel envious; they were happy, radiant, yet they had not chosen each other themselves, and had been married according to traditional criteria.

May that at least make us doubt some of our convictions and attract our attention to how fragile the fascination of love is—so intense, but alas, so rarely able to withstand life in the couple.

There are two types of sexual attraction. The first is immediate, surface sexual attraction. There are ten women on a café terrace where I am drinking a glass of fruit juice; out of the ten, I find five attractive and I find one very attractive. I would like to make love with her, if conditions permitted. And then there is another attraction which can lead to the summits of erotic life. It is an attraction which will never stop growing and indeed which happens when the five other criteria are satisfied, an attraction which comes from one's depths and no longer only from surface fascination. The body of a woman and the body of a man are receptacles of love by which we feel loved, and they are receptacles of a whole wealth of understanding and feeling. It is this aspect—no longer just physical but also emotional and even spiritual—which expresses itself through sexuality.

To the extent that the former sexuality tires quickly (which accounts for the tragedy of male and female Don Juans), the latter sexuality never stops enriching itself through all that has been lived and shared.

If you look back and reflect on them, each of the five criteria cited above is the stimulant of a sexuality which will lead, with ease, to fidelity. There is an element of attraction: this woman perhaps has legs or breasts that are more attractive than those of my companion, but I know that even if I were to have sex with her, it would inevitably be less rich; it would be disappointing—even derisory—because that whole background of comradeship, confidence, respect, sharing, gratitude and memories would be missing. They are two different approaches to sexuality. One can be very strong, until the other—which can be lasting—has taken the main place in our being and therefore in our existence.

Of course, you live in a world where marriages are not arranged: you choose your partner. It is normal that a certain physical attraction come into play; each has his own subjective sense of beauty and charm. But that cannot be the essential aspect in the sexual life of a lasting couple. And attraction based on purely physical, erotic attributes will never lead to more than limited sexuality, whereas if these five criteria are fulfilled, there is the certainty of a more and more rich, profound sexuality which will definitely grow through the years.

These are two completely different lines of life and fulfillment. You cannot try to reconcile them. If you are badly situated within yourself, you have the choice between repression, wearing away, lassitude, habit or adultery—none of that of which you dreamed. But if you are situated within the heart of yourself, the intensity of sexual life is guaranteed by the very fulfilling of these five criteria.

I will repeat them once more so that you can hear them again together, because, after all, they are surely unfamiliar to you.

"The feeling of no longer being alone," of being two companions who share each other's existences, differences, common tastes, friendship and complicity.

"At-ease-ness": no scenes, no tragedies. Everything flows easily. There is even a grace in certain couples: as soon as they are together everything unravels, everything smooths out, all goes well. And there is a sort of curse over other couples: everything grates, nothing works out, as soon as they try something, it fails; they do not understand each other, it is a perpetual misunderstanding.

"Two natures which are not too different": complementary, yes, but not too different.

"Complete trust and confidence in the other." She cannot hurt me; he cannot hurt me. Like a little child with absolute confidence in his mother. I am not saying that you should have a childish attitude towards your husband or your wife; but you can rediscover the heart of a confident child. And after all, Christ said: "If you do not become again like little children, you will not enter the

Kingdom of Heaven." May you feel complete confidence which
feels no need to be wary, to be afraid or to protect itself.

Lastly, "A strong impulse to make the other happy": finding one's happiness in that of the other. If this impulse is reciprocal, if each one finds his own happiness in that of the other, then
both are obviously fulfilled.

If you are somewhat familiar with this teaching, you will feel
that these five criteria—so simple, so true and so complete in themselves—are no small matter, and indeed that the very presence of
the mind, of the projections of the unconscious, emotional vulnerability and fear go against these criteria. And the truth is that, save
rare exceptions, a lasting couple can only unite two human beings
who are sufficiently adult.

There are couples who are happy—certainly so—and yet within
which the husband and wife are not fully adult, show signs of
immaturity in other areas, or even share a complementary immaturity. The latter are those neurotic couples which psychologists
and psychoanalysists are so afraid will be destroyed by analysis,
because their relationship is based on two corresponding neuroses. But such couples cannot constitute a Way of growth, or fulfillment.

To "do" in any domain, one must "be." You cannot do beyond
what you are. If you are a swimmer, you can swim; if you are not
a swimmer, you cannot swim. This is also true in more subtle ways.
One of the great illusions of the human being is that he tries to
change his way of doing, without changing his being. You cannot
change your way of doing without changing your being, but you
can at least change your being—though it be only slightly—and your
way of doing will inevitably be changed because of it. In order to
change one's being, one must first understand oneself. You will not
change what you have not seen, what you do not know, and what
you have not understood.

In other words, a maturity, a wisdom, a little less childishness, a little less emotional vulnerability are necessary for a successful life as a couple. And the illusion that some have dragged
along all their lives, is to believe that things will change if they
themselves do not change, to believe that it is possible to lead a

successful life as a couple—like in their dreams—while continuing to be led by their minds and their emotions.

He or she who still values love and who, until now, has been disappointed by existence, can seriously ask himself or herself: "Is this not a result of what I am, and consequently of the manner in which I am forced to express myself in a love relationship?" There exist genuine neuroses of conjugal failure which lead one to indefinitely repeat the same behavior. For ten years now, I have seen certain individuals making exactly the same mistakes, almost year after year. Every year there is another partner; every year it is a failure, and the reaction patterns are identical.

To realize these five criteria, you must have already surpassed a large part of your coarsest emotions. He or she who is motivated not by the desire for professional advancement, success or money, but rather by the desire to find love—real love, love that lasts—should understand that the first step is to change enough in order to be worthy of such an encounter. One must prepare oneself. In the past, education prepared you, society prepared you. Conditions were much more favorable. Today we are in an era of destruction and disintegration forseen two thousand years ago by the "Vishnu Purana" which, in a famous passage, calls this among other things: "the day when the cast will be mixed and the family itself will be destroyed."

You must admit that you have been badly prepared to be a man face to face with a woman, and a woman face to face with a man. Yet as long as you content yourself with hoping to find love without changing yourself, you will go from failure to failure. So what, first of all, is required of you? Increased earnestness and vigilance in your effort to understand yourself and become free of your mechanical behavior. The whole of what we call Swâmiji's teaching, as I share it with you day after day, prepares you to make a success of the concrete relationship of one individual human being with another individual human being.

A couple relationship, seen in the light of what here we call "the Way," becomes a yoga in itself . . . a yoga which can be completed by the parent-child relationship. There is definitely a yoga of the mother and a yoga of the father.

In this respect, the expression which for me dominates all the words I heard from the mouth of Swâmiji on this theme was *"to grow together."* First, one through the other and then, one across from the other. That is, it is not to be forgotten that although in essence, man and woman both are the "human being"—in the manifestation, man is male, woman is female and there is a difference.

Recently a correspondent sent me an extensive newspaper article from *Le Monde* on the latest studies in brain physiology. It explained that a discovery was now accepted as valid in scientific circles—contradicting what had been considered scientific these last thirty years—to the effect that there is an indisputable difference between a man's brain and a woman's brain . . . without the male brain showing any superiority over the female brain, or vice-versa.

Although man is to rediscover within himself the female dimension of Reality, and woman is to discover and fulfill within herself the male dimension of Reality, this does not make man any less essentially male, nor woman any less essentially female. To discover and understand WOMAN through his wife, is, in itself a Way toward inner growth for a man. The beauty of a couple is that they complement each other. This is far from a passionate love affair without tomorrow. Yoga for two takes time.

Through vigilance, it is possible to see one's reactions of non-adherence to what is: refusal, judgement . . . and little by little, to enlarge one's being to the dimension of one's spouse, and to enrich one's understanding of all that a woman can bring to a man and of all that a man can bring to a woman. It is a case of admitting that a man can both teach much to a woman and that he can learn much from a woman.

Here, Hindu tradition is eloquent. There are numerous relatively technical or allegorical texts which show how the husband is the guru of his wife, and the wife the guru of her husband. But rest assured that if Swâmiji's five criteria are fulfilled, all else will come to you in addition. You yourself will feel that your being is evolving, transforming and becoming more understanding, thanks to the welcome of the female nature—or the male nature—of a given human being with whom you have chosen to unite.

A man who has not been able to fulfill within himself the female dimension of existence is an incomplete man; a woman who has not been able to fulfill within herself the male dimension of existence is an incomplete woman.

It is not sufficient to consider that "we complete each other because I am male and she is female, and we reconstitute the original hermaphrodite." The Way of the couple goes further. It is not just: "I remain a man, she remains a woman and together, we complete each other." No. It is through her that I attain the plenitude of the human state; through her, I understand and fulfill within myself all the female virtues. It is through him that I become a total human being; through him, I accomplish, perfect, and bring all the male virtues to completion within myself. Within each human being, everything exists in seed-form, in the latent state. But everything does not come to maturity. This is a point on which we are led to reflect all too little, living as we do in a world where one hears mainly of conflict between men and women, of a phallocratic society, of women's liberation . . . but much less of this full stature of man and woman.

In couples especially such as those I knew in India, he or she who remains after the death of the wife or the death of the husband, seems to blossom even more. This is a point that surprised me.

At the beginning of one of my old films for television, you see a businessman in his office in Bombay, and then later in the small consecrated room of his apartment (the puja-room or private chapel), worshipping together with his wife. They are neither very young nor very handsome and they would surely not have been chosen to play the tragic love roles of Tristan and Iseult (celtic legend of middle ages) in a film, but for me—twenty years their junior—they embodied success in this domain.

Certain friends had even remarked to me: "If his wife dies before him, Vasudeva will be lost, they live in such osmosis with each other." A while after my return to France, I learned that his wife had just died; a few months later, Vasudeva wrote to me, saying he was coming to France on business. He was a very pious Hindu whom I had often met at the ashram of Ramdas and at that of Mâ

Anandamayî, but he was also a businessman. I was expecting to greet a wounded man, amputated from the woman who had seemed to be his soul, his life—yet I saw him coming through customs at Orly Airport in Paris looking particularly cheerful, fulfilled and almost rejuvenated. In the car, we spoke of Mâ Anandamayî, of Ramdas, of the latest news of the ashrams, and then on arriving at the apartment, I started: "So here you are in Paris again . . . " and he retorted: "Yes, for the first time I can finally bring my wife to France and make the trip with her."

I felt a moment of embarrassment, thinking he was beginning to rave a little. He was probably still normal in his factory, but when it came to his wife, such a great love shattered, he was not able to cope. I was completely mistaken. He continued: "Yes. You know those stupid Indian regulations that you can only get around through corruption, and I would not lower myself. An Indian woman can only get a visa to go abroad if it is for business or for health reasons. But I do not need my wife in my business, and she does not need an operation by a surgeon in London; I was therefore never able to take her with me when I came to Europe. Each time I felt—she is not with me, she is still in Bombay. And now, well, she is no longer in Bombay. She is no longer in Bombay three weeks ago nor in Bombay a month from now when I return, she is living in me. This is the first time I feel that I am taking her to Paris, that I am no longer physically separated, and it is the first time that I have the feeling I am traveling with her." Perfectly sensible words. He had interiorized what had initially been exterior to him, in the physical form of his wife.

I really understood Vasudeva the day when I heard over the telephone—at the Bost in October 1974—"Swâmiji is dead." Before that, Swâmiji was either in Bengal or in Ranchi (where he was taken during the monsoon) and he was in "last June" or "next January." At the very instant when I learned of his death, he was no longer in Bengal or Ranchi, nor in last January or next June. Since then, Swâmiji is everywhere I am, Swâmiji leaves me no more. All that embodied Swâmiji and that I had felt as exterior to me, I felt within me. Today I could say: I no longer live as I myself, but Swâmiji lives within me. But since Swâmiji was not someone distinct from me, this is not alienation—on the contrary. It is finally myself who lives within me, instead of a network of emotions and projections.

Swâmiji's death made me understand Vasudeva's words. Here was a husband and wife who were so united and who, with the wrinkles of age, embodied the perfection of the couple, yet the moment when death shattered their couple did not leave Vasudeva feeling that anything was missing. All that was once exterior to him was henceforth within him. Vasudeva himself had become the totality of them both.

"Growing together"—which, you may be certain, is not possible unless these five criteria are fulfilled—is also growing together in your relationship with others. Ourselves only—ourselves and others—others and ourselves—others only. In no case can a true couple personify what, in French, is called "shared egoism."

Yet there is a risk. If the frustrated child within us (who has such a need to be loved) remains all-powerful, then he will condemn us to shared egoism. I want my wife to take an interest in me, and I am jealous of all those in whom my wife is interested. And vice-versa: I want my husband to show an interest in me and I am jealous of all those to whom my husband devotes himself. A father who has not attained the plenitude of the adult state can be jealous of his first child, especially if it is a boy. Until that time, his wife has lived only for him and now it seems that she lives only for the baby. This is unbearable for most men who, consciously or not, hate their first child at the same time as they love him. This hate sometimes gets the upper hand, and a father can be totally unjust and incomprehensibly hard with his oldest son. Swâmiji affirmed this to me and destiny has indeed given me the chance to see it proven strikingly since the start of the Bost experience.

As long as a man remains fundamentally childish, he needs to feel that he is everything for his wife, just as a little child is everything for his mother. Couples who could have developed and grown have been destroyed by this childishness. Me—me—me—me. No: ourselves and others, others and ourselves. It is entirely different. Love others through your wife, love others through your husband, enlarge this love to the dimension of universal love.

One of the familiars of our ashram one day had the courage

to make a deeply true remark: "As long as I am trying to win a woman's love, to conquer her, I act in a perfectly normal manner . . . few emotions, quite well-situated in myself, relatively adult. But once that woman who attracts me says 'yes,' answers my love, pronounces the words 'me too' or 'I love you,' inevitably and in spite of myself, I become childish, piling error upon error. How is it possible? I have ruined perhaps three loves during my lifetime and I am now in the process of ruining the fourth."

I was able to show him the very simple but so powerful mechanism of the child in us. As long as a woman has not said "yes" to him, she does not yet represent that for which he is searching: the exclusive relationship of the little child with the mother who lives only for him. She is another, she is a woman, he is a man, and he tries to seduce her, to convince her. But deep within the unconscious, there subsists this demand of the child who wants to rediscover that exclusive relationship with his mother, or perhaps of the older child who was dethroned by his little brother and who is searching everywhere for the kingdom from which he was exiled. At the very instant when the woman says "yes" for the first time, he reaches the goal and it is this attitude of the child which immediately takes the upper hand. "She loves me" means she lives only for me. But naturally a woman who loves a man does not have the intention of being the mother of a one-and-a-half year-old child. And so, *things* go badly, *things* are spoiled, *things* are ruined. I have had many examples of it right before my eyes. And when I looked at my past life in the light of Swâmiji's teaching, I saw that I did not have far to go to find examples of this mechanism.

When a man wants a woman to live for him alone, and a woman wants a man to live for her alone . . . and when this is called true love . . . it is true love condemned to perish before long. When a man and a woman, together, open up to others—when the man can find joy in feeling that his wife goes towards others with love, and the woman can find joy in feeling that her husband goes towards others with love—then the couple is destined to grow, then it can no longer be ravaged by emotions.

This is not easy . . . simple, but not easy. I myself made mistake after mistake; I suffered, I was disappointed, I felt betrayed,

I hurt others, I learned, I progressed. And afterwards, over the past ten years, I saw men and women—so very many—hoping for a long time, thinking they had found it . . . and suffering. I have seen the same laws in action—and the same mistakes. I will simply tell you this: if you value the couple and love, then let that be one more stimulant to put into practice all that you have heard and understood of the teaching, so complete and so concrete, handed down to us by Swâmi Prajnanpad.

8

THE COUPLE

I would like to say more about the couple and marital love. You do not need to come here to hear what you can read in countless marriage counseling or psychology books. But if I use other language—with words which stem from a different mentality, a different world, a different society from your own—as Westerners, you will find it difficult to accept. This mentality is so different from our own that I wonder if it really is possible for you to put these truths into practice at the different stages of your lives. Young people, with their married life still ahead of them, may feel directly concerned. Older people will perhaps have a better view of their own lives and the way in which their marriage has unfolded. Of course the perspective here is that of the Way—of surpassing duality and effacing the ego—truths with which I hope you are becoming progressively more familiar.

Marriage plays an essential role in India. Marriage and couple relationships hold a considerably more important place in Hindu society than they do in modern Western society, where many people live together without being married and the divorce rate rises every year.

For centuries, marriage has been a religious celebration. Secularism is a recent phenomenon in the Western world, but the very nature of marriage in the West is not as sacred as it is in India. It is true that St. Paul compared man's love for woman to Christ's love for his Church. But we do not directly consider marriage to be a spiritual path, whereas there is no doubt about it in India— marriage is even a type of yoga. On the other hand, we are not here to imitate Hindu society, nor do I intend to give a conference on the Hindu attitude towards love.

As you know, effacing duality (reuniting the male element and the female element, the two polarities) plays a fundamental role in effacing the ego. A married man and woman can no longer say "my" house—it has become "our" house. Going from *me* to *us* is thus a first step. The ego expands and the sense of separation decreases. The "ego" is the separated sense of individuality, cut off from the rest of existence. The words you have often heard me say about children (not "this is my son" but "I am his father") are words which primarily apply to husband and wife. Not "this is my wife" but rather "I am her husband." Not "*I have* a wife" but rather "*I am* a husband." But they must not be just words! How can you apply them to your own life?

"I am his wife" is the attitude of love; "this is my husband, this is my wife, I have a husband, I have a wife" is the attitude of possession. We rarely distinguish love from possession. Generally we mistake both for love, but they are two opposite attitudes. It is difficult to make this clear to someone who is suffering from too many demands, too many fears, too much painful childishness.

For the sake of clarity, I will use the word "wife" to designate the female partner in a couple, and the word "husband" to designate the male partner.

Although a person can certainly marry at the age of forty or fifty, usually it is a case of a young man or woman who has lived alone up until then. He or she has had a realm of relationships: a child with his parents, a brother or sister in the family, a friend, a student . . . But a much deeper and totally new relationship is about to begin.

In fact, those words "*I have* a wife" or "*I am* a husband" apply to all relationships. Every relationship can be seen either from your personal point of view (where the other should do what you expect, satisfy you and not disappoint you) or else from the standpoint that it is you who exists for the other (trying to understand and see what you can do for him). Educating a child is basically the attempt to make him feel this unselfish attitude. How can his upbringing encourage a child to have a less selfish attitude towards his brothers and sisters, his father and mother, and his slowly-expanding world? A baby's field of interest goes no further than Mom; later it extends to Mom and Dad . . . progressively to Mom, Dad and the rest of the family . . . and finally he leaves the family. This is the beginning of a new stage.

But as yet, the young girl is still a woman (not a wife) and the young boy is still a man (not a husband). Marriage should transform a woman into a wife and a man into a husband. To be a husband or wife is a *dharma*. It is primarily a question of *being*, from the Hindu perspective in its true and therefore universal form. An individual, an egocentric being, becomes a person through a relationship . . . until the relationship itself is surpassed when the person discovers non-duality. But the first stage is to change from an egocentric individual into a person—that is, one who goes beyond his selfishness, enlarging his intellectual and emotional spheres of interest to include more aspects of reality. The normal procedure— the great *sadhana* in this sense—is this meeting of man and woman which, starting from male-female attraction on all levels of nature, transforms this attraction itself into a specifically human phenomenon, a way to attain the full stature of Man.

Therefore two individuals, who started to become persons through the relationships they had while growing up as brother/ sister, son/daughter, continue becoming persons (no longer individuals) by uniting themselves and their lives to a complementary being: the husband for the woman and the wife for the man.

Marriage as an institution definitely fulfills a social function: it provides a family background, indispensable for the growth and education of children. They are future adults and it would be totally selfish not to consider them. But, as I have said, marriage is also sacred—especially in India where everything used to be sacred. (Of course there are exceptional beings who have no need to marry, and go straight into a monastery at the age of twenty. But that is another subject.)

Here we come to a point difficult to understand today, because it is a reality which is growing constantly farther from our current world and customs. It is the question of marital fidelity. Even our Western view of marriage, as presented by Christianity for two thousand years based on verses from the Gospels and certain words of St. Paul, was founded on fidelity. Yet this fidelity was often betrayed. Literature glorifies the woman, married to an unattractive old fogey, who receives her young lover at night; it praises the female conquests of the triumphant or defeated hero. We have come to consider marital fidelity as a narrow, middle-class virtue. I am not talking about aberrations—like money marriages in a perverted society as denounced by Moliére. But the majority of Musset's plays are based on marital infidelity. And aside from the dream of eternal true love which can make the heart of a twenty-year-old skip a beat, this notion of marital fidelity is rarely experienced, or even understood. We are surrounded either by examples of marital infidelity or by couples who have remained faithful but whom we would not like to resemble because they only represent two associated, parallel destinies—lacking intensity and depth.

Yet instead of seeing fidelity as a limiting, depriving and frustrating exclusiveness—externally imposed on us in the name of some moral code—we could consider it as a self-evident and enriching experience. Fidelity is only truly possible when the very idea of infidelity seems impossible. Otherwise, it implies a certain degree of discipline, renunciation, sacrifice and repression which leaves us neither unified nor happy.

I am not saying that it is only possible to be faithful if the thought has never even crossed your mind that another man or woman could attract you. What I am saying is this: fidelity becomes possible if the thought of putting that attraction into concrete form, never even occurs to you . . . if infidelity seems so much outside the nature of things that you do not even consider it.

Personally, I had trouble understanding all this. But I wanted to grasp exactly what Swâmiji was saying because this was something I was beginning to take seriously. It was no longer a case of vague talk. I wanted to understand the real nature of love, which is supposed to bring so much joy yet ends up sowing such suffering and disappointment. Then I thought of a comparison which could only occur to a city-dwelling Westerner. However, Swâmiji approved of it. I am sure it will surprise you at first, so before judging, try to listen with an open mind.

I lived in Paris at the time and, since finding a parking space is difficult for all Parisians, I used to search through all the neighboring streets for a place to park. There were hundreds, thousands, of cars in Paris; but in my pocket were the keys to a certain one—and only that car was mine. There were others which were more luxurious or faster but, not being a thief, the idea of taking any car other than my own never occurred to me.

In India, a young man and woman are often married by family astrologers and gurus—not according to mutual choice. Ever since childhood, the young girl has been preparing herself to be a wife rather than to have a husband . . . and the young man, to be a husband rather than to have a wife. They each understand: "Here is the spouse which destiny or karma has reserved for me"—and they do not imagine anything else. The young man can see that other women may be better singers or better musicians than his wife; the young woman can see that other men may be physically more handsome than her husband, but it is the same situation as the man who knows that, out of the thousands of cars in Paris, only one is his.

The thought of being unfaithful seems out of place. Such a clear and definite sense of exclusiveness at the beginning of life together is what permits a real and deep marital relationship to develop. If the thought exists in the back of your mind that you could perhaps one day take a car other than your own (should you find a prettier one parked by the roadside), then something is distorted from the start.

I gave much thought to this question, which was painful for me because it was my own life as a man in the flesh and blood (with my own mind, *samskaras*, *vasanas*, and karma) which was at stake. And gradually, through deeper understanding, I managed to see what Swâmiji was trying to convey to me.

A man and woman unite, to spend their lives together and to progress from "I" to "We." You are no longer man and woman, you are husband and wife. This is a new status, a new way of being. If, from the very start of that relationship, you have the clear intention of being faithful, then not only does neither of the spouses think of looking elsewhere, but they do not even think that the other would look elsewhere either. Through the "fatal" aspect of the situation, a new dimension appears. (But you will only feel this dimension if you go beyond your reaction to the term "fatal.") It is over. You are united, you can no longer disperse yourselves. Not because you are slaves to rules, *but on the contrary to permit you to gain a yet unknown freedom.* This is what you are unable to understand. Apparent constraints are always the promise of true freedom; our present so-called moral freedom leads us to become more enslaved to our emotions, our unconscious, our endocrine glands . . . to all you can include in an inventory . . . and to our sufferings.

Absolute fidelity greatly emphasizes the gravity of the dharma of husband and wife. This does not apply to the marriage of two utter egoists who do not care in the slightest about dharma. But I am not talking about such caricatures or the degradation of the couple; I am talking about a rebirth within the couple relationship. And that can only happen if the relationship itself is still alive and respected.

Swâmiji told me that a very deep feeling is born at the precise moment one marries. It is born from the firm belief of the two spouses: I am to be a wife for this man present here . . . he is being given to me; I am to be a husband for this woman present here-- she is being given to me. If I am selfish—she belongs to me. But if I have the sense of dharma, if I have been educated according to the great tradition, she is being given to me and I am being given to her. "This being is now entrusted to me; I am the one who will make him happy or unhappy, who will help or destroy him spiritually." And Swâmiji said *"at once love comes."* How hard it was for me to understand that statement! The newlyweds do not even know each other. Yet, when the extremely complex ceremonies of the Hindu marriage rite are over, when the young man and young girl who have perhaps never seen each other before are face-to-face, *"at once love comes."* You can imagine how strange I found that statement; I reflected on it for many hours at the ashram. Do as I did—start by thinking about the words, until the fire of understanding kindles within you. And Swâmiji added: "Now for the man, only one woman will remain a female."

For the wife, only one man will remain a male . . . her husband; for the husband, only one woman will remain a female—his wife. All other men and women are placed in a particular dharma. Another woman is a sister, a fellow worker, a nurse, a tennis partner or a journalist interviewing you. The same applies to men as far as the wife is concerned. If these other relationships are lived in a right and conscious manner, they are clearly defined relationships.

When a pianist plays the piano, he is a pianist. But no matter how famous he may be, when he is swimming he is no longer a pianist but a swimmer. At each moment, we are situated in space, time and causality. Every woman a husband meets and every man a wife meets, will always be met according to a certain dharma—the dharma of the given moment.

At each instant (if it is a real relationship and not just some formless and untruthful imitation), a husband is no longer able to consider other women as "Woman"—the eternal feminine, attraction, seduction and the vagina. It is over.

This sounds surprising: it is over. A man's way of looking at a woman and seeing her as a "female," is limited to one woman—only one. And other men are no longer "males" for a wife. I did tell you that you would have to listen to some surprising things without immediately reacting!

There is such freedom, such purity in other relationships when the male-female background of seduction, attraction and desire disappears. Only then does every encounter, every meeting, become a possibility for communion and non-duality. You can feel exactly what a journalist is, if you feel her to be just that and no more—a journalist who is interviewing you—a "human being" and no longer a "woman." On the other hand, for a husband, his wife will represent all women, all possibilities that the word "woman" implies. And for a wife, her husband will represent all possibilities that the word "man" implies. A wife is simultaneously mother, daughter, sister, friend, associate, mistress, witness and counselor for her husband. She is even a guru who can tell him certain truths which are difficult to hear because they challenge his ego, his world and his mind.

One woman alone embodies all the riches of Woman; one man alone embodies all the possibilities of Man. "We become everything for each other." Both in Indian epic literature and in other less famous works, there are wonderful stories about couples: stories which describe for the Hindu the perfection of Husband and Wife. In our culture, we are nourished on love stories of Tristan and Iseult or Romeo and Juliet, rather than on tales which praise the dharma of marriage. This makes for a strong cultural difference.

It is up to the husband to respond to the demands of his wife. And it is up to the wife to fulfill the expectations of her husband. Although a wife is mother, sister, daughter, friend, associate and guru for her husband, she is also his mistress. In a letter in English on this theme, Swâmiji wrote *"a courtesan,"* and in another letter *"and a prostitute."* That is a strong word. The purest woman should be capable of playing for her husband whatever role a man's imagination finds most sexually exciting. On the other hand, a Hindu wife would find it intolerable to think that she could sexually excite another man. There was great chastity in the India which was true to the dharma. Meeting many Hindu wives of all ages made that clear to me. It goes without saying, of course, that what has just been said about a wife also applies to a husband.

***

This ramification of roles applies to concrete situations. At each moment, a couple is living out either one or another of these relationships. If "conditions and circumstances" permit the husband and wife to have sexual relations, then during that very moment they are lover and mistress, with all that is implied in those words. But if a husband is playing a tennis match with his wife, then they are tennis players. They are no longer lover and mistress, brother and sister, father and daughter, or mother and son. All possible relationships contained in a couple—between one woman and all men, between one man and all women—can be concretely experienced, at each moment of the day. And each one is therefore pure, genuine and complete.

A surgeon is a surgeon when he is operating. When he is swimming, a surgeon is no longer a surgeon—he is a swimmer; when he is walking, he is a stroller. This is very important to remember in order to understand a couple relationship. There are different facets to existence, different forms of being. Yet it is this multiplicity, this variety, which creates the true wealth of life in a couple. There is not just the relationship of husband and wife, there are ten relationships branching out into a hundred different possibilities. Fidelity or monogamy becomes possible because there is neither boredom nor frustration, but *infinite* wealth.

If you are visiting a museum with your wife, you are obviously not lover and mistress. What is your relationship? You are two art lovers, two partners in a particular activity. All relationships, all forms of being, should be experienced in a perfect manner—here and now. This is where we come across one of the great obstacles on the Way: we are never perfectly here and now. We mix up past and future—what we should have done this morning and what we will do tonight. Everything is confused. If you visit a museum with your wife during your honeymoon—even if you are young, passionate and in love—you are an art lover. Mixing everything is no longer being anything at all; it is no longer *being*. At every moment, each relationship within the couple is specific, original and unique. Every situation in your life together as companions, here and now, can be experienced without interference from the mind and without mixing up dharmas. Mixing situations in this way ruins a couple relationship—not to mention the neurotic forces which, through some fascination, mutually attract people who are incapable of getting along, or the fact that today's so-called adults lack inner structures. After a while, a weariness settles over the relationship, the intensity in which you placed such hope fades, and each partner starts to look around outside the couple.

A young man and woman are convinced they love each other: they are sure it is true love and that it will last forever. They get married and leave on their honeymoon. But during the honeymoon itself, the couple will be potentially destroyed—and the destruction will be complete within a few years. It will lead either to divorce or to getting old together without mutual fervor. Or, on the other hand, two entire existences will start off on the right path. This can only happen if there is a certain amount of form, structure, unification and presence within the Here and Now. Instead of being carried away by the mutual fascination of love, this will allow the two spouses to have the right attitude within the reality of each moment, to accomplish the dharmas of the day together, moment by moment. What are your roles when you are having breakfast together? Lover and mistress? Definitely not—you are consumers eating breakfast. You may say: "Listen, I didn't go on my honey-moon to eat breakfast . . . I've been doing that all my life!" That is where you are wrong. May you truly eat breakfast with a companion who is also eating breakfast in a perfect manner. You are *together:* man and woman, male and female. And if each of you has breakfast as perfectly as possible, it will be the preparation for a miracle—yes!--a miracle compared to the usual life of lovers. An hour later, you go shopping (I am deliberately choosing trivial, simple, commonplace activities). You are a customer and the woman by your side is a customer. Be customers together in a true manner. If these little life situations could be lived out perfectly each time, it would be a revelation for the couple, an unexpected discovery. Within a few days, you would feel the wonder of an inconceivable wealth of relationships.

All these roles, which are the continual expression of Supreme Reality, make up the day; they make up the reality of life together. Unfortunately, the habit of always being a slave to impulses and emotions means that all these roles and moments are confused. And this is where the mistake lies.

On his palette, an artist squeezes out a little crimson, a little vermilion, cobalt blue, Van Dyck brown, burnt sienna and Veronese green. If you decide to mix them up and smear everything together (as most children do), there will be only one color left, which will have lost the sparkle of the others—a dirty, dull, dead grey. This is too often what couples who think they are meant for each other do. In a trembling voice, they say: "I was born to meet you . . . you are the one I have always been waiting for." But after a short while, this mixing up so quickly impoverishes the immense wealth of all possible relationships that only habits remain. If you are really ill, with a very high temperature, and your companion takes care of you, then she is a nurse, and vice versa. If you can play the role of nurse and patient well together, it will further enrich your palette.

It is true that an artist can mix certain colors, but he does so consciously. Or else he is a genius in abstract art, like the famous Boronali donkey who smeared canvases with his tail, and was a great success at one of the exhibitions of the period. Just as an artist can voluntarily mix certain colors so too, in a couple relationship, a person capable of certain inner bearing can deliberately combine certain roles in a meaningful way.

***

Try to get a simple view of this trip you are undertaking together. You are either two machines controlled by their impulses or two progressively more conscious, more vigilant beings. All of what is called "the Teachings" or "the Way" is ultimately a preparation for this meeting between man and woman. And if your upbringing was incomplete, if it was badly handled by a father and mother whose own frustrations led them to neglect their children or if you have not met a guru, what will happen? As you know only too well, lack of understanding will lead to the interplay of action and reaction.

This couple, traveling through life together, may be very much in love. But it is also possible that there be a large element of infatuation and compensation in their love, and that two neuroses simply fit well together. There is a way of being "madly in love" which is only a reaction to psychological situations, a reaction to previous chains of cause and effect. And if you let yourself get carried away, there will inevitably be an opposite reaction. If you swing a pendulum too far to the right, its own momentum will swing it just as far back to the left. That is a law which we may as well realize and no longer forget. Yet when the pendulum inevitably swings in the opposite direction, the two lovers are at a loss. Their dream of perfection is broken. There is disappointment, a painful wound, reproach from the other, and the relentless game of clashing emotions . . . just like billiard balls which are hit wherever a pool player wants, not where they themselves decide.

All laws dealing with emotions (pleasant or unpleasant) apply to couple life and to the meeting of man and woman. And certain truths should not be forgotten. No matter how well two beings suit each other—even if an astrologer comparing their charts declares that they were made for each other—there is no such thing as an alter ego. By nature, as of your first encounter and from the very beginning of your relationship, the other is different from you. He lives in his world and you live in your world.

If "I have a wife, this is my wife, she is for me," is too strong a feeling inside you, then you are inevitably expecting certain behavior which even the best of wives could not take upon herself. She cannot be identical to you in all ways. And vice versa. It is necessary to be very vigilant in this, and to remember that "the other is another." "If there are two, two are different." Saying, "I love you . . . we love each other" cannot do away with that law. It should in no way discourage you but inevitably, in certain respects, the other will not correspond to the demands and expectations of your ego.

If you undertake this experience firmly established in your ego, expecting it to be satisfied, the situation is doomed from the start. Remember: not "This is *my* wife," but rather "I am *her* husband." "I am One with her." That is how you will avoid the poison of emotions, disappointments and frustrations. Of course this attitude works both ways. It is simply applying Swâmiji's teachings to a particular situation: the couple. But even the most cunning mind cannot escape that truth. And therefore the mind—no matter how cunning—will not win.

I remember how surprised I was one day, while talking to a typical little Hindu girl, in a typical Hindu family. The child spoke English well and called me "uncle," as is the custom in India. (Every man who comes into the family is called uncle by the children, so that they will immediately establish a personal relationship with the newcomer.) Well, that little ten-year-old girl, whom "uncle" had asked what she wanted to do later on, began explaining: "Later on, when I am a wife . . . " I had not yet met Swâmiji, but that statement already struck me as surprising. It was not, "Later on, when I have a husband, he will take me to the restaurant and he will take me out in his car," but rather "when I am a wife." And she began telling me of her dreams, and that when her husband gets tired, she will massage his legs. I was troubled, moved. Where did I stand? What world did I come from? What was I feeling, standing there beside that little girl who was explaining to me "when I am a wife, and when I am a mother . . . "? This was an entirely different upbringing from "when I have a husband, he will do all this for me . . . "

It is right that this feeling of being and not of having (a feeling of love, not of possession) should have grown gradually within two adolescents preparing them to live a right relationship one day, as man and woman. It is not a case of always wanting the other to be one with you, but of trying, yourself, to be one with the other. In this way, *the relationship*—made up of *the relationships* of each moment—can become truly harmonious.

Most Indian couples have dedicated themselves to the religious Path; they are convinced of certain truths concerning inner transformation and the quest for the Atman or God. So their relationship is not only right from the human point of view, it is further enriched by the spiritual dimension. Marriage is considered an important aspect of religious life and the woman is called upon to play an important role in the ritual life of a Hindu couple. One of the many Sanskrit names given to husband and wife is "partners in the dharma." What is this Hindu dharma? It is an entire existence which includes the dimension of what is sacred: celebrating domestic rites, staying with sages, going on pilgrimages, and searching out the company of seekers of Truth (*satsang*). The deepest husband-wife relationship can only be experienced within this religious setting, which is not one of bigotry but rather of inner growth, awakening and deepening—a pathway toward mystical experience and Liberation.

If this religious dimension and the marked distinction of dharmas from moment to moment are experienced in the right manner, the couple relationship rapidly takes on a certain richness, quality and depth. Each of the spouses feels its undiminishable wealth, unfading quality, and bottomless depth. Instead of becoming repetitious, worn out and wearily familiar, the relationship can only progress. It is either one or the other: love diminishes and deteriorates, or grows richer. Nothing is fixed in this ever-changing, phenomenal world. Both husband and wife intensely feel the wealth of their life together as two companions. Existence is composed of a series of situations, day after day, from morning to night. There is nothing else. Like the Way of wisdom, love is only experienced in the particular, never in the general but in sharing breakfast or shopping together at Woolworths.

I will not dwell upon the ritual aspect proper to India, where much importance is given to rites, and certain rites are celebrated together by husband and wife. But even in the Western world, if you are committed to a path of evolution, you can certainly understand what a great help it can be if your wife or husband acts as a guru for you. If mutual trust is complete, it becomes possible to open up totally to the other, without unconscious protection or fear. The only relationship which can be (or can gradually become) as rich and as perfect as the relationship with the guru, is that between husband and wife. And apart from the relationship with the guru, it is only with his partner that a man can have the courage to show himself as he is; it is only with her husband that a wife can have the courage to show herself as she is, knowing "I will not be criticized, I will not be pushed away; I will be loved, understood and helped."

Swâmiji drew my attention to the fact that, even in a prudish and chaste country like India, husband and wife show themselves to each other completely naked physically. They no longer conceal anything from each other, including the parts of the body which are normally hidden in India. (A woman never shows her legs—at most her feet and scarcely her ankles. And except when bathing in a river or pond, she does not undo her hair for any man other than her husband.) It is important to show oneself completely nude to one's husband or wife, but the nudity of the subtle body should also be total. A true couple show themselves naked to each other, not only physically but also psychologically. And a true husband should be able to lovingly assume the emotional world of his wife.

If you feel "this is my wife" or "this is the woman I love," you will find it unbearable for her to have emotions. If you feel "I am her husband" or "I am the man who loves her," on the contrary, you can accept it. And vice versa. In a right union, you do not need to hide what hurts you or what upsets you; even if, when you are with your spouse, you feel an emotion of which you are not especially proud, he or she can understand it. If you do not impose permanent childishness on your partner, may you be completely accepted—as you are—by him or her, just as you feel accepted by your guru. The couple—the feeling of "we" instead of "I," the home—becomes the place which allows you to face the rest of existence; it is the place where you can have an emotion without its falling back on you in one manner or another. The wife and the husband can each be a guru for one another. And instead of closing up and defending yourself, you let the armor around the ego and the mind be pierced, and you listen to the guru.

***

Sexual equality is very badly understood nowadays. The best way to have a fulfilling life is through classical marriage. This is not how we understand life today. And in the name of Women's Liberation, people make a great mistake. It is quite difficult for me to say this, since I am a man and will be accused of being a male chauvinist, but right observation (focused on hundreds, even thousands of years and not on three hundred years in the West) will lead you to doubt a large number of our present concepts on the emancipation of women. If you can accept what I have said today, then perhaps you can sense this or feel it in a new way: life in the couple or marriage (not as a legal institution but as fifty years spent together) is an essential element of existence, one which is increasingly misunderstood today. Even if they have successful careers or accomplish great feats in life, a man or woman whose marital life is a failure has missed what is most important. Spiritually speaking, being husband and wife is a greater dharma, a much greater yoga, than being an engineer, an artist, a director or a doctor. A man is much prouder today to be able to say that he has succeeded in his career than that he has succeeded in his couple life. Unfortunately for all of us, a man we take seriously is one who declares: "I am commander of the Legion of Honor, I have founded four companies, I was chief of cabinet for a minister and later became senator . . . " And we smile at one who prides himself upon succeeding in his marital life. Well it is too bad for us, for all of us

Westerners. We are so intelligent and so brilliant with our marvelous technology—but so unhappy. Suffering is everywhere in our countries. It was not everywhere in Afghanistan before the Soviet troops arrived, nor in India apart from the misery found in the outskirts of a few large cities.

Life for the couple is not just an emotional demonstration. It is a *sadhana* which should be experienced consciously, a way by which a man becomes a husband, and a woman becomes a wife. And the woman can help the man become a husband just as the husband can help the woman become a wife. It takes understanding, awareness, patience, fidelity. It takes love.

The goal is to advance together toward Liberation. One day, the relationship between "two" is surpassed, in the transcendent consciousness of Non-Duality. "We have become one" becomes true, a reality. The husband is inwardly permeated with his wife and the wife is permeated with her husband. If the separate dharmas of the artist's palette mentioned earlier have been experienced in the right way, Unity reveals itself. There is a beautiful Indian saying which struck me: "And now I no longer know if she is a woman and I am a man, or if I am a woman and she is a man. I only remember this: there were two souls, love came, and there became only one." Separate individuality cannot imagine such unity before experiencing it.

If you understand this message of days gone by, your inner attitude undergoes a complete change. The idea of monogamous fidelity no longer seems to be a social constraint designed only to guarantee a home for the children (which, in fact, is true). Fidelity becomes a blessing which allows you to reach a personal flowering far superior to even the most intense ordinary satisfactions. This will be true even if until now you have felt that there was not just one interesting woman in the world, but many (blonds, brunettes, cheerful ones, profound ones, musicians, seductresses) and likewise, that there was not just one, but many interesting men in the world (intellectuals, sportsmen, artists).

Where do you stand in relation to what has been said here? If you are young lovers or newly-weds, you can understand it in your own manner. If you have a few years of experience behind you, you can see what you have been like; you can recognize your mistakes and throw a new light on your own destiny. Understanding is always liberating. Others who, after divorce or separation, still hope to succeed in a married life which went wrong in their youth, may discover that they do not have to not start again in the same way, according to the same inflexible laws and the same emotional mechanisms. And if you are older, if you are not destined to marry, or if you have decided to live alone—you will meet a younger boy or girl on your path who is starting off in life with many illusions, much misunderstanding and very little preparation. When one has caught a glimpse of what a fulfilling couple life could be, compassion arises for all who are suffering and whose love life has been so frustrating, if not heartbreaking.

Considering what is truly adult in this traditional view of the couple, the countless conquests of male or female Don Juans no longer look like such precious and enriching experiences. Being the mistress of an artist, a businessman and a diplomat is only enriching on the horizontal level, it does not deepen and elevate you. It is a wealth on the level of having—of having multiple experiences— but not on the level of Being. In the end, it is only a sign of childishness.

These truths are difficult to hear and cruel to say. Perhaps I would not have given the same talk, had I myself not had the courage to open up to this aspect of Swâmiji's teaching, and so to see the extent of my own ignorance, childishness and emotions. Whatever has not been fulfilled remains a demand—one which is perhaps repressed, but not surpassed.

In Europe, I have only met very few truly harmonious couples . . . most often deeply religious ones, sincerely and truly religious. If the sacred dimension does not reign over a couple—no matter how romantic they may be and how much they may dream of true love—their love is doomed to dry up gradually. In India, marriage is a spiritual path just like becoming a hermit in a cave or a monk on the roads . . . a path toward Liberation, toward surpassing the ego, destroying the mind, and reuniting oneself. It was always as a guru that Swâmiji spoke to me of marriage—and it was always in connection with the great Goal.

9

THE UNION OF THE SEXES

Sexuality is a theme which has often been suggested to me, but it is one which I have often postponed. It is not easy to break away from clichés like women's right to orgasm and approach the subject in relation to the Way of liberation.

Despite the fact that the sexual revolution is a constant topic of magazines, our modern world is definitely not coping well with it. My own relatively limited experience has shown me that the sex lives of the majority of men and women are not very fulfilling. And even if one has quite a normal sex life, it is still far from what it could be if vicious mechanisms did not interfere.

This word "vicious" has nothing to do with what are commonly called vices—a word we readily associate with sexuality. It refers rather to disturbed mental, emotional and physical mechanisms: distortions, inner knots, and lack of understanding which bring about much useless suffering in an area which, on the contrary, should be purely happy. Why does sexuality—which is meant to be a source of fulfillment, joy and pleasure—bring so many frustrations and clashes, so much dissatisfaction?

We said earlier that the entire Manifest is based on bipolarity: positive and negative, active and passive, masculine and feminine, inhaling and exhaling, taking and giving. If there are "two," two have a certain relationship: attraction and fear, or attraction and repulsion.

The fact that there are two means that there is space, because the two are in a certain position in relation to each other. The fact that there are two also means that there is movement—and movement creates time. In every movement there is tension toward a prospective goal; all movement unfolds through time. So to say that there are "two" is to evoke space and time. The Manifest unfolds in these two categories, perceived by the five senses and conceived by the brain. The means nature has put at our disposal do not enable us to directly perceive atoms and particles.

All human beings, both male and female, are subjected to this natural law. Within ourselves, we carry the two poles: positive and negative, static and dynamic. Male and female values are universal, cosmic. They go far beyond the human species, beyond the difference of the sexes.

The aim of the yogi is to rediscover original Consciousness within himself. This is the point of departure and the point of arrival, or the alpha and omega to use the celebrated expression of Teilhard de Chardin; it is what Indians generally call *aviakta*, the unmanifest. This unmanifest is a state of balance in which there is no tension, a state of peace which can be discovered in deep meditation and in the different levels of *samadhi*. This deconditioning is not like going into and coming out of meditation—it is a definitive discovery which lights up one's entire perception. The surrounding world becomes truly relative, losing its power of fascination and terror, attraction and repulsion.

Whatever Path he follows, the spiritual seeker returns inwardly to the Origin, to what is Beyond (or rather Beneath) the Manifest. This is the return to what is beneath duality, beneath that tension which exists when there are two poles. Hindu masters call this *balance* or *equilibrium*. It is a state of serenity similar to rest, a self-sufficient plenitude, a return to Non-Duality.

The original movement of the Manifest brings about duality or bipolarity. This metaphysical, theological principle rules over all natural phenomena. In human beings, bipolarity can be distinctly seen in the difference of sexes, starting on the physical level (the woman's vulva and vagina, and the man's penis). That is simple and obvious. Why has the bisexuality of the human species brought about so much fear, judgment and condemnation? Why has it brought about such excess, whether it be licentiousness and debauchery or the self-imposed repression and torture of misunderstood and badly assumed sexual abstinence? Sex is the fundamental natural activity. It should be appreciated for its cosmic, metaphysical value. It is the manifestation of a universal law which rules over the macrocosm and the galaxies, as well as the infinite minuteness of the atom.

A yogi tries to escape this natural law of the Manifest, in order to return to the Origin or the Unmanifest. Human sexuality is but one of various means to rediscover one's inner plenitude, completeness and balance.

It is necessary to fully recognize the importance of sexuality, if only because we were born from two sex cells: the ovule and the sperm. After fusing, these two cells divided, specialized and branched out. Since all the cells of the human body originate from the egg, there is no cell in our bodies which does not have sexual origin. But you must try to listen with virgin ears to these concepts. Otherwise images, memories, and emotional echos relating to sexual intercourse will surge up in the background. Sexuality has so often been misunderstood, repressed and denatured that it is the root of almost all neuroses.

Let us remain on natural, healthy ground, concentrating on that sexuality which can easily and unhesitatingly be associated with esoteric ideas and the highest spiritual accomplishments.

There are two ways to rediscover one's original, inner, non-dual condition, without disregarding the sexual bipolarity of our human species. One way is to transmute sexual energy. This is what yogis, monks and ascetics have attempted. Suppressing ordinary sexual activity, however, should not be considered a particular moral virtue. True holiness is unselfishness and love of one's neighbor. Sexual abstinence should be considered a science, a technique, a method. You cannot go about it in a haphazard way. And the other way to rediscover one's original condition is through a perfectly normal and fulfilled sex life ("perfect" in the sense of complete, accomplished).

Undoubtedly, for Christianity as we know it, sex has always represented a certain uneasiness. Various quotations from Saint Paul have led to the severe judgment of sex. It was seen as a human weakness, an attachment to the flesh which was only acceptable when sanctified by the sacrament of marriage (and often then in the sole aim of procreating). But I wish only to state a fact—not to judge Christianity.

This suspicion of sex did not exist in India. It was not because the ideal of chastity or celibacy did not attract Hindus, but rather because sex was seen as a specific path of inner transformation and awakening. It is a well-known fact that the outer façades of many Hindu temples (not just the most famous ones in Khajuraho) include erotic sculptures. These sculptures, which could even be considered pornographic, seemed outrageous to Westerners. However they are found on the walls of respectable temples and are not exclusive to one of those small Indian sects which explore all possible means of self-experimentation.

***

The following are four brief passages from the two most voluminous Upanishads: the Brihadaranyaka Upanishad and the Chandogya Upanishad. These are not Tantric texts recognized only by certain schools, but the very foundation of the entire Hindu Vedanta. Notice how freely the Upanishads—which are spiritual, mystical and metaphysical texts—refer to sex and sexuality.

The first is a basic passage showing how One became "two": "He, verily, had no delight. Therefore he who is alone has no delight. He desired a second. He became as large as a woman and a man in close embrace. He caused that self to fall into two parts. From that arose husband and wife. Therefore, as great sage of the Upanishads, Yajnavalkya used to say, this (body) is one half of oneself, like one of the two halves of a split pea. Therefore this space is filled by a wife. He became united with her. From that, human beings were produced."

You can see that this text, which could be commented word for word, applies to man and woman as well as to the supreme theme of the Creation of the world (the appearing of bipolarity in the Non-Manifest). But I will not go into a long commentary, my aim is to help you feel the spiritual atmosphere of the Upanishads.

The second passage deals with the supreme state, in which one is free from suffering, desire and fear: "As a man when in the embrace of his beloved wife knows nothing without or within, so the person when in the embrace of the intelligent self knows nothing without or within. That, verily, is his form in which his desire is fulfilled, in which the self is his desire, in which he is without desire, free from any sorrow."

The third passage also comes from the Brihadaranyaka Upanishad, but it is found almost word for word in the Chandogya: "The woman, verily, Gautama, is fire. The sexual organ itself is its fuel; the hairs, the smoke, the vulva the flame, when one inserts, the coals; the pleasurable feelings the sparks. In this fire, the gods offer semen. Out of this offering, a person arises."

This passage can also be taken as a literal description of the sex act or it can be considered to be an image of initial reality. Hindu doctrine constantly joins different levels of reality and affirms that the same principles apply to all states, from the most subtle to the most concrete.

The last quote concerns the famous word "Om," and comes from a well-known passage of the Chandogya Upanishad: "This pair is joined together in the syllable "Om." Verily, whenever a pair come together, they fulfill each other's desire." The word for sexual intercourse, *maithuna,* is found twice in the Sanskrit text of this little quote, but it does not immediately stand out in the English translation. Therefore the syllable "Om" is also clearly being compared to sexual union. I repeat that I have chosen these quotations because they come from two major Upanishads and not from less important ones associated with only a limited number of Indian schools of thought.

How are you to understand these quotations? In the Manifest, a state of imbalance must exist in order for there to be movement. Otherwise everything would return to inertia. If there were total inertia (if the dance of the particles in an atom were to stop, if the planets were no longer to turn around the sun), if movement were to disappear—then time and space would also disappear. The interaction of attraction and repulsion is found in all forces. If the two trays on a weighing scale are motionless, there is no latent energy in the scales. But if you take one of the trays off the scales, the other will immediately fall. Through that up-and-down movement, action and reaction, the latent energy in the trays will bring them back to inertia.

Nature strives endlessly toward rest. But through the laws of cause and effect, action and reaction, new impulses are constantly provided to once again disturb this rest and inertia. This, on all levels, is how the Manifest unfolds. No matter the tradition to which a spiritual seeker belongs, he tries to go within himself to find what escapes movement, impermanence and incompleteness. Within himself, beyond time, beyond eternity or the eternal present, beneath multiplicity—he tries to discover that which is full in itself, complete in itself. This is Ultimate Consciousness. In the Vedanta, it is called the Atman—the Self.

***

Sex can be regarded as a spiritual path in itself. Psychologists and psychotherapists agree that sex is a desirable accomplishment, but it is also as a way of surpassing our conditioned and limited human consciousness—with its desires, fears and dissatisfactions.

Let us look a little closer. All human actions are two-sided actions—generally alternating ones. For example, we inhale and exhale, but we cannot inhale and exhale at the same time. That is why yoga breathing exercises sometimes include prolonged periods of holding one's breath, either after inhaling or after exhaling. During those periods, you neither inhale nor exhale.

This is one very important biological instance when the rhythmic action of breathing, which is life itself, stops. It is one way of returning to the Unmanifest. When breathing stops, thinking also stops. You can each observe this. It is easy to have no thoughts if you stop breathing, but a multitude of thoughts assail those who try to meditate in one way or other.

Human existence is composed of the two-sided movement of giving and receiving. Sex entails the two aspects of the Manifest—active and passive—for both the man and the woman. To understand this, you must come back to an obvious but too often forgotten reality. Before being a man or a woman, we are all human beings. Since the word "man," which means human being, also designates the male, there is some confusion. There is so much insistence on the difference between men and women (on what a "real man" is, and what a "real woman" is) that we forget something much more important: we are first of all "human beings." Then comes the essential, undeniable difference between the male and the female. But spiritual teachings are intended for human beings; the Upanishads are intended for human beings.

When the Teachings mention the *koshas*, they mean the *koshas* of the human being (which are neither male nor female). When the Teachings speak of the supreme Self or *Atman*, it is the Self or *Atman* of a human being. And we are all meant to achieve the perfect completeness of the human state. Normally, we are just seeds; we are unaccomplished and unfinished human beings. This is the fundamental idea behind the Gospels, and behind all spiritual teachings.

We are sown on Earth at a given level. Nature will make us into adults, with the possibility to fertilize and reproduce. But nature will not turn us into human beings in full flower . . . sages. This *perfection in the relative world* will come as the fruit of our own efforts, according to the tried and proven methods of the different spiritual paths. Even with the aid of a guide or guru, this achievement will still come only as the result of our own perseverance. We should never lose sight of this, even when we are speaking about sexuality.

We must realize that there are two general categories of human beings. First, there are those who are satisfied with living as nature designs (full of fears, desires, and sometimes a large amount of generosity and courage), but who are not driven by the stable and constant desire to transform and liberate themselves to attain the full human stature of Wisdom, Awakening, Liberation. And then there are the much less numerous ones, who have taken charge of their own evolution, and perfection. These are the ones who have committed themselves to a Way—whether they are Moslems, Christians, Buddhists or outside the recognized religions. Of course this basic distinction also applies to sexual life. There is the natural sex life, dealt with by psychologists and psychotherapists, which is relatively fulfilled or neurotic, and there is the sex life of the disciple progressing along the Way of Wisdom.

Everything said until now applies to both men and women. There are no Upanishads for men only, or for women only. A fully blossomed human being has fulfilled the two forms of the Manifest within himself: the male and the female; the receiving, welcoming, opening side and the active, intervening side. These two movements are perfectly balanced within him. Individually, he no longer feels either the need to receive or the need to give. He has the right to say "I have done what I carried within myself to do, I have received what I carried within myself to receive, I have given what I carried within myself to give." His actions are now spontaneous and impersonal; they respond to the necessity of the moment. He acts according to what the situation requires or through love for others.

But this does not happen immediately. Indeed it will take a long time to become entirely self-sufficient, to be absolutely free of tension, to be desire-free and fear-free (at least free of any desire which would make him suffer if it went unfulfilled, and free of any fear which would make him suffer to see realized). This is freedom, the discovery of the indestructible within ourselves, of unaffected Consciousness, the foundation of the entire Vedantic teachings.

There is a two-sided movement in sex: a welcoming of the other, and a going toward the other. These two forms of the Manifest are more significant and obvious in sex than in any other life situation. Given the difference of the sexes, the first and most obvious fact is that the woman biologically receives the man's semen. Woman has a receiving genital organ; man has an emitting genital organ. No one can deny that, whatever his philosophical, social or political opinions may be.

In sex, it is normal and natural for the receiving aspect to dominate in the female partner, and the active aspect to dominate in the male partner. But more essential than the distinction between male and female is the fact that we are all first of all human beings. Man must also be welcoming and receptive; woman must also be active. Any publications on sex which too strongly accented woman's biological passiveness and man's biological activeness would be deceiving. Although to all appearances, sexual activity itself arose from the difference between the sexes, it is only if the woman can develop her own male dimension and the man can develop his own female dimension that each partner will truly feel sexually fulfilled. Current ideas on sex greatly undervalue, or totally omit, this fundamental fact.

You will develop the right view by simultaneously under-standing two levels: the difference between man and woman, and each one's capacity to become fully human. This means that the man becomes progressively more female, and woman becomes progressively more male. Of course this does not happen because they change their physical appearances, but through the flower-ing of all the latent possibilities within each one. Each rediscovers the completeness and perfection of his original nature. This is the meaning of the androgynous state described by Plato and suggested in the verses of the Upanishads quoted earlier, in which the Di-vinity is compared to a man and woman in most intimate union.

***

A sage like Mâ Anandamìyi or Ramana Maharshi does not need a sex life because he or she is complete. But such people are exceptional. Other human beings are destined to have a sex life; it should not be seen as a means of giving in to the weaknesses of the flesh, but rather as part of the Way—as part of a true Way. I am emphasizing the word "true" so that you will not confuse it with a shallow interpretation of Tantrism, which is a very popu-lar but badly understood word. Much extravagance and sexual ambiguity, experienced without any true understanding, has been decked out in spiritual rags under the name of Tantrism. I there-fore decided to quote four verses from major Upanishads instead of a Tantric text which is so open to interpretation that it can be used to serve our uncontrolled drives, lack of self-control and various other weaknesses.

You must try to merge these two realities: on one hand, the obvious difference between the sexes; on the other, the call to rediscover one's own full stature as a total human being without turning into a "women's liberation" type of caricature.

These two realities must be experienced simultaneously. Try to feel them simultaneously. To be sexually fulfilled, a woman must be truly woman and a man must be truly man. Modern psychol-ogy or sexology can tell you that. But what does it mean to be truly woman? It means fully personifying openness, receptivity and welcoming. Nature shows us that the essence of the sex act is the female reception of the male sperm.

Our modern civilization has fostered a problem which would not be found in a traditional society: women have too often been unable to develop these values within themselves. They have refused them and considered them inferior. They have let themselves get caught up in the game of exaggerated maleness where silence, meditation and contemplation are considered downgrading while action (even agitation), output and productivity are greatly extolled. In essence: when you listen, your attitude is female; when you speak, your attitude is male. Likewise, for sexual harmony to exist the man must have developed his full male stature, his capacity to intervene in the world in order to change or transform it. Many sexual dissatisfactions, many frustrations, failures and sufferings can be explained by the fact that women have difficulty being truly female, and men have difficulty being truly male.

The modern tendency is to try to solve sexual problems without adequately taking the rest of life into account. We ask why a woman is frigid, why a man is impotent, how a man and woman could change their lovemaking techniques, what psychological preparations to make, how tender words, caresses and kisses can prepare a woman for penetration. Much has been written on these subjects, although often the advice does not produce the expected results. Psychologists find it quite difficult to solve sexual neuroses and to bring harmony to couples whose partners do not suit each other.

Let me give you a simple suggestion, although it is one which may be difficult to put into practice. A man expects his companion, wife or lover to embody "woman" for him in a general manner—not only during their sexual relations. And a woman expects her partner to embody "man" for her in a permanent manner—not only during sex. Until you pay close attention to those words "in a general, permanent manner," your difficulties will persist. A man can continue trying to play the male in bed, and a woman can do her best to be extremely feminine in bed, but neither will understand his or her partner, and neither will understand himself or herself.

10

ABSOLUTE LOVE

Let us look together at the most terrible reality of all . . . love. How many meanings can be put into that word! All human existence—with its dramas, tragedies and sufferings—centers on love, because what we usually call love is simply the other face of hate, just as hate is only the other face of love. Open your eyes and look at all that this often-used word encompasses, starting with the child's "I love you" or "I don't love you any more" to its mother.

Both French and English lack the wealth of many other languages (including those of some African tribes) because we have only one word for love whereas others have two or even more. In Greek there are three words, "eros," "agape" and "philos"; Sanskrit uses "moha" for attachment and "prem" for love. You can undoubtedly feel the enormous gap between the "I love you" of lovers (who hate each other six months later), and the love of Buddha or Christ. Ever since childhood we have felt much inner confusion because French and English each have only one word to describe such different realities. "For God so loved the world that He gave His only-begotten Son, so that whoever believes in Him should not perish, but have everlasting life" (Gospel of John). God so loved the world . . . and a little boy like me loves chocolate so much.

What duality? Although the idea is foreign to our modern Western culture, habitual consciousness (with its sense of ego, limitation, and "me" as being different from "the other") can be surpassed; there is a state of non-dual consciousness wherein one no longer feels separation. You realize that "the other" is an expression of yourself. Remember the comparison of one unique ocean with different, separate waves? If a wave thinks of itself as a wave, it will feel completely different from the wave which precedes it and the wave which follows it. But if a wave realizes that it is actually the ocean, then it sees other waves as simply being other forms of itself.

Ordinarily we feel a separation, or duality, between "me" and "the other". One of the Upanishads says: "If there are two, there is fear." That alone is worthy of contemplation. If there are two, or if you feel that there are two—"the other" and "you"—then there will inevitably be attraction or repulsion. This will be expressed through "I like—I don't like," "I want—I refuse," "I desire—I fear" until you return to neutrality. "The other" harms you, hurts you (be it Dad punishing you as a child or some adversary when you reach adulthood), or else "the other" is good to you. But if he treats you well, if he makes you happy, you quickly learn that this happiness is not stable and that the very one who is making you happy, or has made you happy, can also make you suffer—if only by dying. The most perfect and unshadowed love can cause intense suffering if one of the two partners (child or mother, husband or wife) is suddenly killed in an accident.

In a deep subconscious memory, we store recollections which go back far beyond this life and prove how fragile happiness is, when it is founded on the relationship of two. If there are two, it is inevitable that sooner or later two will be separated. That is also a law. Liberation cannot be won by closing one's eyes to universal laws at work. It is only on the metaphysical plane that there are no longer any laws. Only pure Consciousness exists—supreme, limitless, indivisible Reality—escaping our categories of time, space and causality. We can attain this supreme Reality in our own innermost core, in our own consciousness. But such realization is rarely attained. Instead, we remain within duality or separation. This ego sense (me and others, those I like—those I dislike) brings about affinity, hostility, love, quarrels and hate. It is the basis of everything psychologists study; dropping it is what has made Sages free. The law of life, that which spurs you on, is this: if there is love, there is inevitably hate; if there is attraction, there is also repulsion.

So because we have only one word for love, you are confused; you mix up the love of Christ or a Sage with what you yourself call love. To understand the distinction you will have to be much more precise. What you usually call love is an expression of the ego sense, the sense of separation and individual limitation: it is the need to be loved. If we say we are in love with someone, but he or she no longer loves us as we want to be loved, then our love for that person is immediately affected, it is mixed with emotion. You can only really love (in the sense which you give to the word today) once you no longer need to be loved.

Pay close attention to this, for I am not talking about the transcendent love of Ramana Maharshi or Buddha—a metaphysical love which you glimpse vaguely through stories or books. I am talking about love . . . that true love which you long for and dream of, the love which rightly or wrongly is attributed to Romeo and Juliet, to Tristan and Iseult, or a child's love for its mother and a mother's love for her child. But remember that it is only once you no longer need to be loved, that you will really be able to love. Then the other's love also comes to you. But it is no longer a necessity. Once we no longer need to be loved, only then are we finally capable of loving, and can we really feel the other's love because the background of fear has disappeared. You must understand this, otherwise you will always be chasing after idle fancies. You will be chasing after a dream which can in fact be attained (but not under just any conditions), one which never corresponds to what the majority of human beings imagine in their adolescence.

The need to be loved is what defines a human being. Swâmiji one day said to me: "You are a beggar." For those who have lived in India, the imploring beggar, endlessly pestering and following you as he repeatedly begs for a coin, is a much more meaningful image than it is for someone who has only lived in the West. Swâmiji told me: "You are a beggar, you are begging for love." If you are honest, you will see that no matter how much professional or worldly success you may have, even if you are irresistibly seductive . . . you are a beggar, continuously begging for love.

***

When we feel loved—if only for a moment—we no longer feel the fundamental fear of the future. We live in fear because we know that we cannot count on anything. Everything can eventually betray us: health, physical body, career, best friend, husband, wife. Everything can betray us—if only by suddenly disappearing in a war or an accident. We cannot count on anything. But someone who really feels loved no longer feels this fear. You may not have noticed or clearly realized it, but this is true. When you feel loved, the danger of atomic war has not disappeared, the danger of accident has not disappeared, the dangers of unemployment or economic crisis have not disappeared. The impending dangers which weigh upon all of us have certainly not disappeared . . . and yet fear itself has disappeared. When a man and woman are really in love, if for the moment their love is complete and sincere (regardless of whether or not the relationship is destined to last) then fear disappears, even in threatening or tragic conditions. Bombs may be raining down on all sides, but a child will no longer feel afraid if his mother simply takes him into her arms and he feels loved once again. His innate feeling of duality, of separation, is momentarily effaced.

But you also know that perfect love can come to a sudden end. Life joins and separates. One man may be taken prisoner in a camp and not see his wife for five years; another may die, leaving his young wife with four children. Love is the greatest tragedy of all. It is the source of the most "divine" joy for humanity, and it is the source of the greatest suffering and revolt: "If there were a God, He would not have let me lose my son, who was so young, under such conditions . . . " or "He would not have let my wife be killed in that accident."

The need to be loved animates everyone, not only those who are alone in life or whose life is nothing but frustration. Even the president of a country begs for love—his begging only seems to be compensated by success. A politician feels loved by those who vote for him. During election results, watch the emotion with which politicians accept success or defeat—it is an emotion which goes much deeper than their career, an emotion which means "I am loved," "I am not loved" or "I am no longer loved." If you have the honesty and courage to see to what extent you beg for love, then you have already reached a certain stage. Do not judge, do not be afraid, just start by looking at what is.

We demand absolute love. This is our fundamental need, our

absolute need. No one wants to be loved relatively or just a little, we want to be loved in a perfect, total, unshadowed, flawless way, forever. All our experiences of love are measured up against this absolute standard. This is the explanation for so much suffering. You believed you had found absolute love when you met a certain man or woman, but after the first few months of dreams and projections, you discover that your love is only relative. You find yourself across from someone who also needs to be loved, and he or she also demands the impossible of you—absolute love. Your dream of absolute love is shattered, and you find yourself in a relative world which you cannot accept. It is part of being human to carry within oneself this demand, this absolute necessity. Why stop along the road? Why be satisfied with less? As children say: we want the most, of the most, of the most, of the most . . . in other words, infinity.

A human being's demand for love may have been intensified by childhood frustrations, lack of maternal love, or by the mother's death when the child was young; it can come from many conditions and circumstances. It can even come from surprising *samskaras* from past lives—like a nostalgia remaining from a deep love which was interrupted by death. But fundamentally, the need to be loved comes from an ego-based state of consciousness, making us feel that "I" am separated from "the other". The other will always act according to his own personal drives, you cannot depend on him; he will never be a musician obeying your conductor's baton, to use Swâmiji's expression. He will perhaps bring you immense happiness, but he can also inflict knife wounds which will be all the more painful if you placed high hopes on the relationship. You all know this, or knew it once, but you forget; it is a lesson which you do not really understand. A person can fall deeply in love five times in his life, and each time he can make the same mistakes and come up against the same failure.

There is a connection between the desire for love in a man-woman relationship (or in a homosexual relationship) and the desire simply to be loved . . . to be truly loved as the little child in you was at least relatively loved by its mother. Yet I am telling you that you can only love if you no longer have the gut-level need to be loved. As long as you need to be loved, you can not really feel the other's love because you are afraid. In fact, you are doubly afraid: if it fails, you could be hurt; if there is harmony, a tragedy could destroy everything. Emotions and neuroses always interfere in spite of ourselves, so we run after dreams and almost always end up disappointed. No one's absolute demand is satisfied. And yet it is not impossible to be happy as a couple. But it can only happen if you no longer need to be loved, and therefore if you are no longer afraid—afraid of betrayal, afraid of separation, afraid of the future. You must be able to live the present moment . . . perfectly, fully, "here and now."

***

Having been loved does not mean having been loved by mechanical, emotional love; it means having been loved by that other love for which French and English have no particular word. As a Westerner, let me share with you a little of my personal experience, one no better or worse than average. Little by little, I came to understand that meeting sages progressively fulfilled the desire for true love which I, too, projected onto the ideal woman. That may sound surprising—it was from old men that I received the love for which I carried a longing deep in my heart at the age of twenty. It may make you smile, but I am quite serious. Little by little, my need to be loved was fulfilled. I was not aware of it at first. For years, I could never get enough love. I wanted the guru to live for me alone. But in spite of all, I felt loved . . . loved by Mâ Anandamayí, loved by Kangyur Rimpoche, loved by Sufi Saheb de Maïmana . . . people whose language I did not speak, people who were not of my race. I felt completely, absolutely loved.

In 1970 I had acquired a certain television reputation, and one day I was interviewed on the air about the series of films I had done on sages and their disciples. The interviewer, thinking I had decided to specialize definitively in a certain type of film, said: "So you never intend to do love stories," meaning: "You will never do films with a scenario." My reaction surprised many who were watching the program and who spoke to me afterwards. They said I looked stunned: "What! But I do nothing but love stories!" It was a cry which sprang straight from the heart. On hearing that question, I realized that although I had lived in an atmosphere of adventure, mystery, beauty, esotericism and spirituality, it had above all been an atmosphere of love.

Unfortunately saints and sages like these, who give love in the same way as the sun gives warmth and light, are rare in our society. And this is a great loss. As in Europe of old, meeting a sage is one of the most precious essentials of life in the Orient today. People travel hundreds of miles to see a sage, to have what Indians call his *darshan*, to simply remain silent in his presence. Because even if it is the first time in your life that you meet him and he does not know your name, where you come from, or whether you are married or single—at that very moment he loves you with unfailing love.

You can only love, and feel someone else's love, if you no longer need to be loved. And it is only once you have really felt loved, that you no longer need to be loved. I have really felt loved, among others by a man to whom I pay tribute today, a man whose name is well-known, Sensei Taisen Deshimaru, who died recently in Japan. It was not his impressive walk nor the force which emanated from him that made me recognize Sensei as a master, it was his capacity to love. Sensei Deshimaru loved, and I will always be ready to bear witness to that. It makes me smile to hear that he drank too much or that he used to get angry, when he was a man capable of such compassion. I lived three months of my life, day and night, with Deshimaru in Japan. I saw him love children, students, humble people, rich bourgeois from Tokyo, politicians. His unwavering tenderness is what stands out in my memory. Under a countenance so different from that of the frail Ramdas, there was the same love.

Meeting a sage, which plays such a great role in Islam, Hinduism and Buddhism, answers our unquenchable thirst to be loved. Of course going to see sages is not enough to transform one's life. Personal efforts are also necessary. The Way is a whole.

Later I realized that there was one man in particular who had given me love—Swâmi Prajnanpad. I am sure that Ramdas loved me as much as Swâmi Prajnanpad did, and that Ramdas loved thousands upon thousands of others just as much as he loved me. I know that even though I was a non-Moslem Frenchman, Khalifa-Sahib-e-Sharikar had the same love for me as Swâmiji had. But Swâmiji showed his love concretely through tireless patience and attention. That old man gave me much of his time and energy, even when he was frail, ill and liable to die of a heart attack from one moment to the next. He wore me down in the end. His love was so unshakable that all my doubts, fears and projections—all I imagined about him—progressively melted down like wax under heat. One fine day I completely capitulated. A cry of victory arose in me, like Buddha's cry of victory when he announced to the entire universe that he had attained Liberation: "I have been loved!"

These sages give us a love which does not judge. It can be firm, it can even seem severe in order to help us progress—but in fact it never judges. It is absolute love, the expression of the sage's realization of non-duality and inner neutrality. And do not be deceived: the word neutrality is synonymous with infinite love, although that may sound surprising at first. The Sage loves you as you are.

But no one has ever loved us absolutely, as we are. Apart from during those first weeks of our lives when Mom accepted that we wake her up at night and we dirty our diapers, no one has ever loved us as we are. We have been loved for what people wanted us to be, for what they wished we were, for what they imagined us to be, for what they asked us to be. That is why we live in fear. How could we have been the perfect child our parents wanted us to be? But the Sage loves us absolutely, as we are.

At least credit God with being capable of the same love as a guru, with having psychological understanding equal to that of the most well known psychotherapist. A Sage loves us as God loves us—without judging. Especially for us Westerners imbued with Christianity, this is a fundamental card in hand to help us play and win the game of our own Liberation. I said earlier that love was the most terrible reality of all. Now I would like to talk about the most horrible one of all—not loving yourself.

***

Not loving yourself, not accepting yourself as you are, judging yourself, feeling guilty and condemning yourself . . . this is certainly not what Christ, who taught love and salvation, came to bring to the world. But it has too often happened in Christianity. As if God could stop loving! We alone, through our errors, condemn ourselves to hell. If God exists, he is inexhaustible and infinite love. But because our parents stopped loving us for a moment when we displeased them (and we must accept that), because we have been saturated with the idea of good and bad, because we were not able to fulfill the expectations of those whom we admired (grandfather, grandmother, father, mother, godfather, friend, or whoever) we live, or have lived, in the tragic situation of not loving ourselves.

That is perhaps one of the most fitting definitions for the ego. You think that being selfish and ego-centered means loving yourself instead of others. But no—the ego is what makes us not love ourselves. It is because we do not love ourselves that the ego remains and persists. Earlier I said that there are two meanings for the word love . . . two loves, two different realities. This also applies to one's love for oneself. Self-esteem, vanity and sensitiveness are definitely egocentric. But the selfishness or ego-centeredness of which you are unmistakably prisoners is actually a mediocre self-love, since it never stops judging and condemning you. Think about it: the ego does not mean self-love, it means the lack of self-love. You are disappointed in yourself; you refuse to forgive yourself for being no more than what you are. If you had only been quieter as a child (but you were noisy), if you had been more cheerful, more graceful, a better student . . . you would have felt more loved. But you hated yourself for not having all the talent, charm and qualities which would have made you the center of interest of the whole family and of everyone you met.

Even if my hair has grown a little because it has not been cut in a while, you probably realize that I did not have long blond curls when I was young. I do not remember how old I was, but one day I heard someone sing the praises of another little boy who had beautiful curly hair. The result was that I tried to put in rollers at night, thinking that would give me curly hair. When the adults found out, they took the situation rather badly. So by trying to be loved by also having curly hair, I had made things worse. As adults, that makes you smile—but for me as a child, it was an agonizing experience.

Do not forget that the great metaphysical concepts are closely connected to the most ordinary details of life. And do not forget either that a child's sensitivity is not the same as that of an adult's. It is true that so-called adults have childish emotions. You can see this when they buy a sports car or get into a discussion with a neighbor over a common dividing wall. But a child wants only one thing: to feel that everyone loves him. The mind grows up with the child and the mind is woven with comparisons. It hurts a child— it hurts him very much—to hear his cousin's curly hair being praised, to be criticized in public or to hear comparisons which are not in his favor. On the other hand, comparisons which are in his favor take on enormous importance and increase his vanity; he "adds on" to them because they reassure him.

We live in a strange situation, but it is the human condition: inside ourselves we carry a fundamental need to be loved in an absolute way—this is the only way we can transcend fear. On the other hand, we are convinced that we cannot be loved as we are because we are not handsome enough, brilliant enough, agile enough, intelligent enough, admirable enough. How can we forgive ourselves? So life consists in compensating—such sad, pitiful compensations.

With a sense of absolute and infinite gratitude, I can say that (imperfect as I was in the relative) I felt loved by all the sages to whom my films and books paid homage. As I was—awkward, childish, fallible, proud—I was lovable, since Ramdas looked on me with so much love. I also saw and realized what those sages did for me, to help me in my voyages, to be of service to me, to enable me to make those films. Instead of only consisting in fine words, their love slowly filled me with a new conviction, one which was the opposite to that engraved in me during childhood. Imperfect as I was, I could be loved. And little by little, I learned to love myself.

You will never feel loved until you love yourself. Remember: you can only love if you no longer need to be loved. It is only when you no longer need to be loved that you can really feel the love that is given to you, because there is no more fear in the background. And you no longer need to be loved if you have truly been loved by yourself. That is the deadlock in which almost all men and women are struggling: my dream is to be loved, I feel an impera- tive need to be loved, I fail because my love affairs are always emotional (when they are not neurotic). I live in fear, impossible demands, projections and blunders—because not having felt suf- ficiently loved, I am not free of the need to be loved. And I will never be free of that need, until I am able to love myself.

Apart from the guru's love, it is your own love that you need most. You need to love yourself just as you are—incomplete and imperfect. No one can simultaneously be as good a tennis player as MacEnroe, as good a guitar player as Segovia, as gifted in phi- losophy as Sartre, as muscle-bound as Muhammed Ali and as politically famous as François Mitterand. You will never be that imaginary hero who you wanted to be as a child, so that your whole family would love and admire you. And you cannot forgive your- self.

You think you cannot love yourself as you are. That is what distorts everything and turns life into such a pitiful quest for love, into such a failure. And to mask the failures, we hide behind the lies and illusions of the "mind."

I am sure now that this plays a fundamental role in meeting sages. Instead of begging love from those who are incapable of giving it because they themselves need love too much, we go and beg love from those who no longer need to be loved, from those who are totally self-sufficient and are consequently able to truly love. If you are sincere, if you do not protect yourself, you will agree with what I said earlier—it is terrible. It is a terrible tragedy: the hope we put into love, the divine moments of which only bitter- ness remains, the passions which change so quickly into wounds and hate until, to suffer less, we end up destroying the wealth of sensitivity that lies deep within ourselves.

***

We could look at love in purely religious terms: God's love for us and man's love for God in response to His love for us. If we understand these words in an authentic, living way (instead of a narrow-minded one), we can also find truth in the religious approach . . . truth which surpasses the mind and ego of theologians. All that is necessary is an understanding of the deep meaning—I might even say the intelligent meaning—behind the familiar terms of a Christian education.

There exists a Supreme Reality—like the water in each wave of the ocean—which moves us, animates us from within and unites us into one mystical body. There is nothing else but love, on any level: passionate love, disappointed love, betrayed love, suffering love, enticing love, supreme or divine love. There is nothing else but love—whether it be dualistic love, calling out for help ("I'm afraid to be alone"), or love which is the expression of the inner discovery of a non-dependent Reality.

The Sanskrit expression *sat-chit-ananda* (Being-Consciousness-Bliss) tries to give a glimpse of the Reality of ultimate Consciousness. If you go deeper into the meaning of these words, they mean love; they mean absolute love which "understands all, forgives all, and never dies." Absolute love makes everything possible—even for ourselves. *Ananda* (bliss) is self-love. Could there be bliss of any kind if we do not love ourselves, if we refuse to accept ourselves as we are, if we are overwhelmed by guilt?

God loves you as you are. Again and again Christ said: "I have not come to save those who are healthy, but those who are sick," "I wish not the death of the sinner, but his salvation," "Judge not, that you may not be judged." God loves us as we are; Swâmi Ramdas and Khalifa Sahib-i-Sharikar love us as we are . . . imperfect as we are. Are we the only ones who cannot love ourselves? Let me repeat: it is lack of love for ourselves which makes up the ego. Liberation is loving ourselves—at long last.

We are also convinced that our "imperfection" has jeopardized whatever attempts we have made to be loved. With "ifs" the mind has free rein . . . If you were not what you are, your love affair would have worked out. If you were a hero, the woman would have loved you . . . but when she saw you for what you are instead of through her projections, she was disappointed; she came down to earth and your beautiful dream was shattered. And if you were different from what you are, you would be respected by your employees, appreciated by your superiors and loved by your fellow workers. Once more, it is your own fault if you cannot be loved. How can you love yourself? Yet the way to salvation is to "love yourself."

The Gospels say: "You shall love the Lord your God with your whole heart, your whole soul, and your whole mind". This is the great and chief commandment. And the second is like it: "You shall love your neighbor as yourself." On these two commandments the whole Law and the Prophets depend." They do not say: "Love your neighbor, but do not love yourself"; They say: "Love your neighbor as yourself." The supreme meaning of those words is that your neighbor is really yourself. This is what we can discover if we escape limited, individual, separate Consciousness—like the wave which discovers that it is the ocean and that the other wave is itself.

Love is more important than any of the technical aspects of the different *sadhanas*: concentration, meditation, *asanas, pranayama, pratyahara, dharana, dhyana* (in the language of yoga) or being a witness, and distinguishing the spectator from the spectacle (in the Vedanta). The West will soon develop a kind of spirituality in which love has disappeared and only techniques remain. Or it will fabricate a spirituality inundated with sentimental love, full of mixtures, lies and confusion. Psychoanalysts will easily be able to attribute it to nostalgia for a perfect father and mother, or compensation for childhood sufferings. There are forms of spirituality which seem to be full of love but which are actually full of childishness. They attempt only to soothe our childishness and keep us dependent; they do not fulfill our need for love, they do not lead us to freedom.

Perhaps you have come across religious people who often use the word "love." And yet they do not seem to be growing older in a happy, serene, fulfilled, free way, in communion with the entire universe. They have missed the essential: reconciliation with themselves. They have lived a religious life based on love, while continuing not to love themselves; they have tried to love God, while continuing to judge themselves and constantly dragging along a guilt which psychologists and psychoanalysts are only too happy to attribute to a Christian upbringing. We must have the courage to look truth in the face and see the degradation of what we tend to admire or venerate.

However in all non-devotional paths (Hynayana Buddhism, Vedanta, Yoga of Knowledge or the technical yogas), it is essential to recognize man's infinite nostalgia for love, his disappointments in love and his inability to love, to feel loved and to respond to love. You will never be able to relinquish your nostalgia for love. And if you try to smother it through technical exercises of meditation and concentration, you will achieve neither peace nor freedom. Techniques without love are like electrical appliances in a house without electricity.

Physicist, mathematician, Sanskritist and psychologist—Swâmiji was a tremendous man. But in spite of all the admiration I had for him, what remains in my memory is that he was a man who loved. Ramdas the poet and Swâmi Prajnanpad the scientist had one thing in common: love. Theirs was an immense love, an ocean of love. Love is synonymous with Brahman . . . Atman . . . Consciousness . . . Awakening . . . Wisdom . . . Liberation. And love is the source of all hate, all wars, all suffering—because we do not feel loved, because we suffer, and we struggle and we try to escape our fear and suffering.

Someone who really feels loved cannot be mean; someone who really feels loved cannot be ambitious, stepping on others in order to succeed. Never. And someone who has done something important in his life is someone who has felt loved . . . most probably by his mother. There are no mean men or women—neither Stalin (who was responsible for the death of twenty million of his fellow citizens and revolutionary comrades-in-arms) . . . nor Hitler . . . nor anyone else. There are only badly loved people. If Stalin had really been loved, he would not have killed twenty million Russians; if Hitler had really been loved, he would not have killed several million Germans and Allies. And we only have one word to designate all forms of love—from the most pathological (ending up in court with "I loved him too much! That's why I threw sulfuric acid on his new mistress"), to the compassion of Buddha or the love of Christ.

All forms of love actually have a common background. Human drama is this: am I Liberated or not? Do I live on the level of the limited, separate, frightened ego? Or have I attained that of the sage who has discovered God within himself and lives in absolute security (a wealth "which thieves cannot steal and rust cannot destroy")? This selfsame tragedy is taking place in everyone—Hitler, Stalin, Saint John of the Cross—but at different levels of maturity and understanding. The little, limited, mortal wave hopes to discover that it really is founded in the Ocean. "In Him, we live and move and have our being," as Christians say.

***

Love your neighbor as yourself. You cannot love anyone unless you love yourself. How can parents, who have so dreamed of loving their children, behave in such a hard, awkward, thoughtless way toward them? How can a fiancé, who has sworn to love his fiancé, behave so badly toward her . . . and vice versa? How is it that, although we want nothing more than to be able to love, we are all so incapable of loving? For unless you live in a dreamworld, you must see that you are not even able to love your own children.

You cannot love because you do not love yourself, you have not become reconciled with yourself. Include yourself in absolute Love! To be able to give yourself, you must first love yourself—with the same love as you have for others, neither more nor less. But it is so difficult to love oneself with one's limitations, imperfections and mediocrity. You reproach yourself . . . you nurse a destructive guilt . . . you resent yourself . . . you are not proud of yourself . . . you feel ashamed . . . You do not believe that what you are, what you do or what you have done is good. You are stuck in a world where you judge yourself and you judge others. And through your criticism and admiration, you end up reinforcing that duality from which you are supposed to be trying to escape.

Stop judging. Stop judging others and stop judging yourself. Try to love others as they are, and to love yourself as you are; try to understand others as they are, and to understand yourself as you are. Understanding leads to sympathy, sympathy leads to love. This is true in relationships with others, and it is true in your relationship with yourself.

If the other aspects of the *sadhana* suggested here are also put into practice, identification with the ego ("me, myself") will be surpassed. The ego is the veil hindering you from discovering that inner state of unaffected Consciousness which Ramana Maharshi compared to a movie screen on which any variety of film can be projected. As long as you remain identified with the ego, you will not discover Supreme Consciousness; and until you learn to love yourself, you will remain identified with the ego. Supreme Consciousness is an inner fullness which lacks nothing and no longer needs to be loved. Even if you are criticized, hated and slandered— it is no longer of any importance.

Absolute fullness reveals itself deep within the heart. This is the promise of all spiritual teachings. Why should that promise not come true for you? When it happens, slavery to the need for love disappears. And the fear of being hurt by another, or of being separated from someone you love also disappears. It is then that we can love totally, without fear; here, now, in this very moment . . . we can give all our love. Because fear is no longer there in the background, we are able to appreciate and recognize the love which is given to us. And even though that love may be relative or imperfect, but it is still precious for what it is.

When the need for love is too great, you are like a sieve which can never be filled, even if water is poured into it every day. The only ones who can fill the sieves and transform them into saucepans, so to speak, are those whose love is not relative . . . those who love as Sages do. Almost all human love is tarnished by a fear which springs from the compulsive need to be loved. So everything is distorted.

Love and fear cannot exist at the same time. You can be in love, be infatuated, commit suicide or commit murder on a background of fear—but you cannot love on a background of fear. And this background of fear is really the deep, unconscious fear of being once again disappointed or betrayed. At the slightest sign that the other is another, that he is different from you, all the old wounds awaken. You feel: "He doesn't really love me" . . . and up spring all the unconscious mechanisms studied by psychologists. Why drag your life (perhaps even a series of lives) into a pursuit which is doomed from the start?

Change yourself, transform yourself; if your being changes, your destiny changes. *"Your being attracts your life."* One day you will attract the partner who corresponds to your nature, with whom you will be able to harmonize in the relative world, someone you can meet without fear. Welcoming what is unfavorable as much as what is favorable, truly experiencing the cruel aspect of life—without denial—leads one to the discovery that suffering is not painful. When you know deep down inside that you have the power to suffer no more (even in painful situations which may once have been agonizing), your confidence illuminates every encounter with the opposite sex: "He can help me but he cannot hurt me."

If you are afraid of the other because he or she can make you suffer, then unconsciously, deep inside, you will not forgive him. At the very moment you think you love him, you will simultaneously be hating him because you know that he has a power over you: the power to make you suffer. But if fear disappears, you have nothing to lose. You can give yourself completely, here and now. And if you are sufficiently stable, steady and emotion-free to awaken in the other a progressively increasing free consciousness, he may also understand that he too can play the game. Then love becomes possible.

If you are no longer afraid of not being loved, it becomes possible to love and to feel loved. Otherwise even when someone is ready to offer you a love which could grow and deepen with the experience of life, sharing and communion, as soon as "the other" does not correspond to what your mind expects, you feel betrayed, stabbed. You suffer, you react emotionally—and then you yourself begin destroying that in which you placed your hopes for happiness. If you have been in love (and rare are those who have not been, at some time or other), then you know how vulnerable and fragile the need to be loved makes you. Someone who is free from the neurotic conviction of not being loved, does not feel simple forgetfulness as betrayal; he can understand that it is not so serious. It does not mean that the other no longer loves him, it is just the other's way.

We cannot believe that another human being can love us and that his mind functions differently from ours. If I feel that "she" should write to me, and that if "she" does not write it means she does not love me, then she is hurting me and the suffering I feel forces me to react. But if the fact that she does not write arouses no fear in me—if it does not blind me and carry me away with emotion and thoughts generated by emotion—then I can *see* that the woman does indeed love me, but that she is different from me. The next time I see her, I will not be feeling wounded, reproachful, bitter and full of hate . . . (yes, full of hate, because we cannot do otherwise than hate someone who has caused us to suffer). You can see each other again without fear. You can be relaxed and approachable; you can have a new outlook with the knowledge that only the mind could have fabricated a full-fledged betrayal, an utter disappointment, which actually did not exist. Even the true love of your life will never be a replica of yourself.

If we no longer need to be loved in order to feel that "we are" and to be able to escape fear, then love—human love—is also given to us. Do not think that you will only have access to the transcendent love of a monk or hermit who loves all humanity from the deepest recesses of his cave or monastery. You will have access to serenity, to unfathomable peace, to *sat-chit-ananda*. You know this, you have heard it, you have read it. But you will also have access to that human love of which so many dream, yet so few really discover. The way of Truth is not only austerity! *Be happy.*

BRIEF GLOSSARY
of Sanskrit terms used by Arnaud

ahamkara: the ego, awareness of oneself as a separate individual;
    "I am me"(separate from others).
ajnani: one who is ignorant.
amrit: immortality, supreme bliss.
ananda: bliss, peace, happiness; self-awareness.
ardhanareshwara: Hindu sculpture which is half male, half female.
asana: posture.
ashram: a community of disciples.
asti: it is; it is so.
Atman: the Supreme Self, the supra-personal state.
aviakta: the unmanifest, a state of tensionless balance, a state of peace
    which can be experienced in deep meditation.

bhoga: the conscious fulfillment of acknowledged desires; true
    appreciation, real experience.
buddhi: non-subjective intelligence, right vision, objective view in
    situations.

chakras: the subtle energy centers of the body.
chitta: the psychism (a person's entire unconscious, the depository
    of all his or her memories—both conscious and unconscious);
    the storehouse of all one's samskaras, i.e. all the latent tenden-
    cies which one carries engraved within oneself.
chitta shuddhi: purification of the psychism.

darshan: sight (seeing a sage, a divinity).
dharana: concentration.
dhyana: meditation.
Devi: goddess; woman who has attained an exceptional spiritual
    level.
dharma: the right order of things, divine law, universal law, scien-
    tific laws. ("That which supports and maintains the world.")

hara: Japanese word for the center of gravity in the lower abdomen.

jnana: knowledge.

karma: action. The law of cause and effect. The totality of a person's actions including the consequences of those actions. Personal destiny.

koshas: coverings of the self:
-physical
-physiological
-mental or emotional (psychological)
-objective intelligence
-personal bliss

lingam: a phallus; famous vertical black stone sculpture; symbol of shiva.

lying: (English word with no corresponding Sanskrit term) Technique developed by Swâmi Prajnanpad for the purification of the unconscious; a plunge into one's unconscious in order to consciously live out unconscious trauma.

maithuna: the sex act, sexual mating.

maha bhokta: the appreciator: one who has real knowledge of the totality of existence, appreciating both sides—the pleasant and the unpleasant.

maha jnani: the great sage: one who has true knowledge.

maha karta: the great doer: one beyond the sense of individual ego, who no longer reacts but instead truly acts.

manas: the mind, as the basis of egocentric thought and false perception of reality. (At times, one's entire psychological manner of functioning.)

manonasha: destruction of the mind.

maha: illusion, attachment.

Om (Aum): amen, yes, acceptance; sacred syllable, symbol of Brahman.

Prakriti: the female principle, Nature; that which is Manifest.

pranayama: mastery of energy through breathing techniques.

prem: supreme love, free from any trace of selfishness.

puja-room: private chapel in a home.

Purusha: the male principle; the Unmanifest; the conscious witness. the fulfilled man. The universal man.

sat-chit-ananda: being-awareness-bliss; Buddha nature, the Self.

sadhana: the path, the way, spiritual discipline, conscious effort in view of liberation.

samadhi: ecstasy, supra-individual consciousness, being "one" with all.

samskaras: subconscious latencies or tendencies, the weight of the past, deep impressions proper to each individual.

satsang: the company of spiritual seekers.

Shakti: the female principle; the dynamic aspect of Shiva. Fundamental or divine energy. Cosmic energy.

Shiva: the male principle; the witness, the immutable. God of destruction and death; the Benevolent.

upa-bhoga: false, impulsive, mechanical appreciation of things; the more or less unconscious fulfillment of desires which are not fully recognized; (experience which does not help one to progress along the spiritual path).

Upanishads: Hindu texts of wisdom.

vasanas: needs, unsatisfied demands, fears, desires, latent tendencies (to redo, relive and re-experience what has already been done, lived and experienced).

yoni: a cup; femininity; the supporting cup-like base of the lingam.